STAND
OUT

STAND OUT

How to Find Your

Breakthrough Idea

and Build a Following

Around It

DORIE CLARK

PORTFOLIO / PENGUIN

PORTFOLIO / PENGUIN
Published by the Penguin Publishing Group
Penguin Random House LLC
375 Hudson Street
New York, New York 10014

USA | Canada | UK | Ireland | Australia | New Zealand | India |
South Africa | China
penguin.com
A Penguin Random House Company

First published by Portfolio / Penguin, an imprint of Penguin Publishing
Group, a division of Penguin Random House LLC, 2015

LIBRARY OF CONGRESS CATALOGING-IN-PUBLICATION DATA
Clark, Dorie.
  Stand out : how to find your breakthrough idea and build a following
around it / Dorie Clark.
    pages cm
  Includes bibliographical references and index.
  ISBN 978-1-59184-740-3
  1. Creative ability in business.   2. Career development.   3. Success in
business.   I. Title.
  HD53.C562 2015
  650.1—dc23
  2014038643

Paperback ISBN: 9780593853894

Set in ITC New Baskerville
Designed by Pauline Neuwirth, Neuwirth & Associates, Inc.

147141878

To Joel Gagne and my godson Seamus—
men of character

CONTENTS

STAND OUT

Introduction

You have something to say to the world. You have a contribution to make. Each of us has ideas that can reshape the world, in large ways or small. It might be developing a new business process, creating a new literary movement, or finding a new way to deliver humanitarian aid. It could be changing how the world looks at a political cause, or how students are taught, or how the corporate world should handle work-life balance. Whatever your issue, if you really want to make an impact, it's important for your voice to be heard.

Yet too many of us shrink back when it comes to finding and sharing our ideas with the world. We assume the leading experts must have some unique talent or insight. We assume that our own ideas may not measure up. We assume that working hard and keeping our heads down will be enough to move our careers forward. But none of those things is true. Most recognized experts achieved success not because of some special genius, but because they learned how to put disparate elements together and present ideas in a new and meaningful way. That's a skill anyone—with hard work—can practice and learn. And more and more, it's essential. In today's competitive economy, it's not enough to simply do your job well. Developing a reputation as an expert in your field attracts people who want to hire you, do business with you and your company, and spread your ideas. It's the ultimate form of career insurance.

It's overstating the case to claim that there's a surefire formula for becoming a recognized authority in your field. But are there patterns? A common set of principles that almost every respected leader follows, consciously or unconsciously? Without a doubt. With hard work and smarts, almost any professional *could* become a thought leader in his or her company or field. Few ever try—and that's your competitive advantage. If you're willing to take the risk of sharing yourself and your ideas with the world, you're far ahead of the majority, who stay silent.

You were meant to make an impact. Now is the time to start.

BECOMING A RECOGNIZED EXPERT

Let's get clear on definitions. In this book, I'll be talking about how to become a recognized expert—a thought leader—in your field. First, if you are a *thought* leader, you're known for your ideas. If you have celebrity without intellectual content backing it up, you might as well be a reality TV star. Kim Kardashian, whatever her other virtues, is not a thought leader. Second, you must have followers in order to be a thought *leader*. Being an expert is great, but it's not sufficient—it merely implies you know what you're doing. Thought leaders strive to make an impact, and that requires them to get outside the ivory tower and ensure that their message is accessible and actionable. It's also important to note that you don't need to be the world's leading authority on a subject; you can be a thought leader in your company or in your community as well.

Recently there's been some cultural blowback about the concept of "thought leadership" itself (a term coined in 1994 by Joel Kurtzman, then the editor in chief of *Strategy + Business* magazine, regarding thinkers whose ideas "merited attention"[1]). In a *Harvard Business Review* article, Sarah Green pushed back on the notion, asking, "Don't we have enough ambitious workers leaning in so far that they're toppling out of their desk chairs? Enough 'thought leaders' selling dubious credentials and platitudinous advice? Do our workplaces really need more ladder-climbing, cheese-moving self-promoters?"[2]

The underlying assumption seems to be that aspiring to the creation of new and important ideas is somehow sleazy, or a form of strategic puffery. Admittedly, some advice on thought leadership is vapid and banal, just as some advice on marketing, or strategy, or finance can be. But sharing your ideas with the world—when done right—is a far more meaningful act. Often, it looks like bravery.

When Diane Mulcahy was hired by the $2 billion Kauffman Foundation to manage its private equity and venture capital portfolio, she realized something was wrong. The foundation had invested in more than one hundred VC funds over two decades, but as a former venture capitalist, she realized the returns were far less than they theoretically should have been. Figuring out what was going wrong was important for the foundation's finances, but also for its mission. If venture capital was broken, the Kauffman Foundation—which focuses intensively on supporting entrepreneurship—needed to understand why.

Mulcahy began investigating, and the numbers weren't pretty. "Venture capital has had poor returns for over a decade, and the analysis we did on our own portfolio showed VC returns had not beaten the public markets, which is a terrible thing to have to say," she recalls. "Venture capital promises to beat the public indexes by a fairly high margin— that's the only reason you'd invest in a private partnership that ties up your money for a decade and charges high fees. It was a very big deal to come out and say, with a lot of data to back it up, that venture capital doesn't deliver on its promises."

Mulcahy's report didn't name names or criticize specific VC firms. But it laid bare Kauffman's own investment portfolio, a striking move in an industry that's generally opaque. She took on the sacred cows of the industry, highlighting the overly generous terms VC firms negotiate for themselves. "VCs go around talking about what great investors they are," she says, "but in actuality, they're paid on fees *regardless* of how good an investor they are." Indeed, VCs running a

$1 billion fund make $20 million a year from fees, even before a single investment is made.

She started facing resistance even before the report was published. "I had at least a handful of people say to me during interviews, 'Diane, why are you doing this? You'll never work in this industry again.' Some people said it in a genuinely personal, caring way, and others said it in a mildly threatening way. There was a sense that if you're going to write things like this, reports that are provocative and go against the accepted narrative, your career in this industry is over."

Once the report was released, the firestorm intensified. Her report was widely discussed by industry blogs and in the news media, but it didn't make Kauffman, or Mulcahy, popular in some quarters. Some asked why they were "killing venture capital" or trying to "make it harder for entrepreneurs to make money." Others questioned whether Kauffman's poor returns were the result of flaws in the venture capital system, or just its own bad investment decisions.

Mulcahy, who subsequently wrote about her findings in *Harvard Business Review*, believes the report started a productive conversation in the industry, but she warns potential thought leaders that shaping the dialogue in your field can be a fraught process. "I received a great piece of advice from somebody on my investment committee," Mulcahy recalls. "'This is going to be emotional,'" he told her, "'and you need to be prepared for that, and for the possibility that this could get personal.' That was a real eye-opener, and he was right: people in the industry reacted emotionally."

When you're a true thought leader, it's not about advancing

you—it's about advancing your ideas. Because of her extensive knowledge of venture capital, Mulcahy understood that Kauffman's returns might indicate an underlying problem with the industry. In saying the emperor has no clothes, she faced an enormous amount of personal and professional risk, but she followed the data where it led. To help other foundations and investors, and to spark a dialogue about how venture capital is done, she shared her research publicly.

Sometimes the process of change can be frustratingly slow. "Don't look for immediate change," advises Mulcahy. Following her report, there are nascent signs that the industry is beginning to shift—VC pitch decks now often list the report's recommendations, and describe how the fund meets them. The premier consultancy in the venture capital field is now starting to track VC performance against the public markets, a Kauffman recommendation. "But let me be clear—they didn't attribute that change to us," Mulcahy says. "People have a lot of entrenched interests, and a lot of inertia, and things take time to change." But eventually, with patience and persistence, they do.

STANDING OUT IS NO LONGER OPTIONAL

Mulcahy's decision to move ahead with the report may seem risky, but sometimes it's riskier not to act. In a world where income inequality is at its highest levels since 1928,[3] the benefits of standing out and being the best—no matter your field—are rapidly increasing. We've shifted much more toward a winner-take-all economy.[4] During the rebound following the Great Recession, a full 95 percent of all income gains went to the top 1 percent.[5] In a world where you can now watch simulcasts of the Metropolitan Opera (instead of buying tickets to regional opera performances) or "study with" superstar professors in MOOCs (instead of settling for the instructor nearby), there's less room for average performers. You can't get away with being the best option at hand; in a global economy, you need to be recognized as the best—period.

Meanwhile, "safe" jobs, predicated on staying quiet and doing what's expected of you, are fast disappearing. There's a lingering cultural belief that if you just work hard enough, you'll be lauded as an authority if your work merits it. Unfortunately, that's a recipe for professional disaster. People are overwhelmed by the clamor of their direct reports, Facebook friends, and Twitter followers; they just aren't paying that much attention to you. As the average job tenure decreases, you can't rely on your reputation as a hard worker; your new boss and colleagues have no clue. You need to be willing to share yourself and your ideas if you expect to advance.

Building a strong professional reputation is the best way to protect, and advance, your career. When you're recognized by others as an authority in your field, clients and employers want to work with you, specifically—and if you do lose your job, you're equipped to bounce back. That's what happened to a friend of Des Dearlove, cofounder of Thinkers50, a biennial ranking of the world's top business leaders. Dearlove's friend was nearly fifty when he got laid off from his longtime employer. But he'd laid the groundwork for a successful landing. He'd volunteered for international conferences, chaired committees, and built relationships with people across his field.

"The shock of being 'made redundant' quickly morphed into the shock of getting offers from all over the world," recalls Dearlove. "They said to him, 'Why don't you set up the UK office of this or that?' Finally, his old company offered him a new job and he said, 'You know what? I've got much better offers now.' He was an international thought leader in his own industry, and that worked fantastically for him in terms of employability and his personal brand. He had standing and status and a reputation that went beyond the brand of his organization." Whether you work inside a corporation or as an entrepreneur, today's challenge is the same: how to add so much value to others that they fight to have you on their team.

To succeed in today's economy, you don't have to be a worldwide superstar, but you do have to be deliberate about identifying the place where you want to make a contribution and starting to share your ideas. The competition is fierce, but if you even begin to develop thought leadership, you'll dramatically outpace your competitors, most of whom never even try.

THE WORLD NEEDS YOU

The ultimate reason to invest in developing and spreading your ideas is—as Steve Jobs put it—the imperative to "put a dent in the universe." Why do you go to work each day? What do you hope to accomplish? What do you want to be known for at the end of your career, and your life? Anyone can go into an office and sit at a computer for eight or ten hours a day. But some people know they're made for more than that. They have ideas—perhaps still inchoate—that can improve their company, or even the world. They realize they won't feel complete until they've made a contribution they can point to: something that's different, and better, because they made a mark.

Whatever your cause, or perspective, or point of view, we can't afford for the best ideas to remain buried inside you. The world needs your insights. Whether it's reducing crime or predicting election results or improving a manufacturing process or stopping spam e-mails, there are an infinite number of ways to make a contribution. We don't have to settle for following orders and keeping to the work we're expected to do. Our value isn't as robots, executing tasks. It's as thinkers, who make connections and spark new insights and change the world by seeing things in new ways.

How are you going to make a contribution? Thought leadership is about a lot more than just making money (though, as we'll discuss, finding a way to sustain yourself is essential). It's not about selling books, or going on the lecture circuit, or schmoozing at elite conferences. It's about solving real problems and making a difference in a way that creates value for yourself and others. True thought leadership is a gift. It's a willingness to be brave, open up, and share yourself. It's a willingness to risk having your ideas shot down, because you genuinely believe they can help others. It's a willingness to trust that your generosity will benefit the world.

MAKING THOUGHT LEADERSHIP HAPPEN

If you want to become recognized as the best in your industry, you'll have to fight for it, but the promise of this book is that your goal is possible.

Early in my consulting career, I tried to get booked as a speaker at a local chamber of commerce. I sent them an introductory letter, a sample DVD of one of my talks, and a packet of information, and dutifully called to follow up. They claimed never to have received it, so I sent it again. In response to my second call, they once again insisted they'd never received it—apparently the party line—and then hit me with the truth. "Why should we book you, anyway?" the director asked. "We have an infinite number of consultants who are dying to speak to our members."

To him, I was a commodity—no different from any other interchangeable speaker they could put behind the podium. I knew I was better than that, but he didn't. I vowed that I was going to find a way to differentiate myself, to make my ideas known, and to ensure that clients and event organizers would seek me out, specifically.

I've spent the past decade sharpening my ideas and attempting to broaden my reach, so I can share them with others. Today, thankfully, I get paid to give talks, and no longer have to grovel to be allowed to do it for free. I teach at business schools around the world; consult and speak for great organizations, from Google to Yale University to the World Bank; and I have the opportunity to share my ideas regularly in publications like *Harvard Business Review*, *Forbes*, and *Entrepreneur*. This book is the result of what I've learned personally, and it contains insights gleaned from interviews with dozens of thought leaders in an amazing array of fields, from genomics to urban planning to personal productivity to high tech. (All quotes, unless otherwise footnoted, come from the personal interviews I conducted.)

In the first section of the book, we'll focus on identifying your own breakthrough idea. Using today's top experts as examples, we'll deconstruct the process successful leaders have used to find and develop their ideas. The path varies; for some, it's developing one "Big Idea," and for others, it starts with a microniche that expands outward. Still others develop unique research that sheds light on their field, or draw from other disciplines to offer a new perspective, or create a framework that helps the world better understand a complex phenomenon. There's no one "right way" to develop your breakthrough idea; any of these approaches can yield powerful insights and generate meaningful contributions.

In part 2, we'll turn to the question of how to build a following around your idea—an equally critical component that ensures it reaches the world. It starts with building one-to-one peer connections: a base of supporters who believe in you personally. The next step is turning outward and developing an audience—a larger group of fans who resonate with your message. Finally, it's about connecting those followers with one another, magnifying the power of your idea and ensuring that it's talked about even when you're not in the room. That's when you've built a movement. In part 3, we'll bring it together and talk about the logistics of making thought leadership happen. First, we'll talk about making the time for thought leadership. Some people, such as university professors, are lucky enough to have jobs that allow them to develop their ideas as part of their regular duties. For most of us, though, that's not the case, so we'll discuss strategies for balancing existing professional obligations with the kind of research and thoughtful contemplation that's necessary for idea creation—not to mention the social media and content development that's required to spread the word.

Next, we'll turn to making a living. If you're not getting paid directly for your thought leadership, how can you make it sustainable? We'll look at strategies that various thinkers have employed, from online products to speaking to mentorship programs. We'll also tackle the critical question of how to make money while staying authentic, so you don't feel like you're selling out or cheapening your ideas. Finally, we'll get real about the level of effort required to distinguish yourself and your ideas. We all know it's not easy, but we'll drill down on the specific schedules and techniques used by various thinkers so we can see what's really involved in getting to the top.

More than ever, for the sake of your career and our society, it's important to ensure that your best ideas emerge and take root. This book will help you develop them—and create the momentum necessary to make sure they spread. Consider this a framework to help accelerate your career, spread your vision, make an impact, and live the life you've imagined. *What's the idea you want to share? And how are you going to start spreading it?*

PART 1

FINDING YOUR BREAKTHROUGH IDEA

YOUR VOICE DESERVES to be heard. It might seem almost impossible to get noticed amid the 1.4 million books published in 2013,[1] the 100 hours of video uploaded to YouTube each minute,[2] and the 500 million tweets per day.[3] But it *is* possible, and in part 1, we'll break down the process by which successful thinkers have been able to find and develop the ideas that have made their name, and made an impact on the world.

We'll start with how to develop **Big Ideas**—the bold, industry-changing insights that most people associate with thought leaders. We'll also talk about cultivating an **expert niche**—a narrow specialty that can provide a crucial toehold—and about the power of **independent research**. We'll look at how to **combine ideas** from various disciplines, a mix-and-match that can take your ideas in powerful new directions. Finally, we'll discuss **codifying a system** to help others better understand complex phenomena.

In today's crowded marketplace of ideas, you need to be able to show others—quickly—why they should listen. By following the templates forged by some of today's top thinkers, you'll be able to coalesce your ideas, show how they're valuable to others, and break through the noise.

The
Big Idea

Einstein's theory of relativity. Gandhi's vision of non-violent resistance. Jung and the collective unconscious. Those Big Ideas upend our beliefs and expectations and make us see the world in new ways. To create them, a genius is struck with inspiration—Newton gets bonked by an apple, Archimedes shifts in his bathtub—and in an instant, it all becomes clear. Right?

The truth is a lot more complicated. Big Ideas aren't hatched by a rare breed of intellectuals living in isolation. Instead, they come from regular people who are willing to ask the right questions and stay open to new ways of looking at the world. To assume that creativity is something that other people do—that you aren't capable of it—is an abdication of responsibility, says Professor David Burkus, author of *The Myths of Creativity*. It's incumbent upon us to open our minds and try, rather than shutting down before we even begin to engage.

True thought leaders are driven by asking questions that others have not, and question assumptions others take for granted. Of course ulcers are caused by stress (an accepted medical "truth" until an obscure Australian doctor shunned by the medical establishment proved—by infecting and then curing himself—that they were actually the result of a bacterial infection[1]). Of course something as high stakes as space flight should be run by the government (until entrepreneurs like Elon Musk and Richard Branson began aggressively creating successful private ventures). And of course the only right way to teach college classes is by having a professor lecture in front of a small group of students (until Stanford professor Sebastian Thrun gave up his tenured teaching position to launch Udacity, an online MOOC provider, after seeing that his first pilot course attracted 160,000 students—more than he could reach in dozens of lifetimes teaching in a traditional classroom).

Finding the next Big Idea is about cultivating a questioning mind-set. It's easy to accept established wisdom—which is usually, though not always, correct. But it's in those moments where conventional wisdom fails that the biggest breakthroughs occur. Thrun had no idea how many students would register for his first class, but when he saw the overwhelming results, he was willing to jump on board and explore. Barry Marshall, the intrepid Australian doctor, couldn't be 100 percent sure of his hypothesis until he drank the *H. pylori* concoction himself, but he was willing to step forward and test his beliefs. In this chapter, you will

STAND OUT

learn how to challenge the implicit assumptions you're making, and test whether something is really impossible—or just difficult enough that most people haven't bothered to look further. We'll examine the importance of asking what's next—a critical question in a rapidly changing world. It's easy to see what's right in front of you, but if you broaden your perspective and think critically about the next year, or five or ten, you can add real value to the conversation. Finally, we'll look at how your own personal experience can lead you to Big Ideas.

WHAT ASSUMPTIONS ARE WE MAKING?

Every field has useful guiding assumptions. Received wisdom saves time—you don't have to reinvent the wheel—and stops you from pursuing fruitless leads, but it can also be a trap, preventing you from exploring new ideas. To find a Big Idea, you have to question the assumptions that are keeping everyone else in check. You don't succeed by following the rules and thinking exactly like everyone else; you need to ask "what if?" and "why not?" Try to put yourself into the mind-set of an outsider, who doesn't know all the rules. What would they make of how things are typically done? Are there practices they might find counterintuitive or outmoded? Might there be a new or different way of doing things? Finding that answer could be the seed of your Big Idea.

That was the case for Robert Cialdini, now an emeritus

professor at Arizona State University. As a young researcher studying influence and persuasion, he ran his experiments the traditional way: bringing research subjects into the lab and running experiments on them. But as he progressed in his teaching career, something began nagging at him. His students would invariably raise their hands and ask how he knew the laboratory results worked in the real world. "My answer was, you have to trust that the findings we're getting in the lab are going to reflect what we'd get in [natural environments]," Cialdini recalls. "The principles we're investigating are the same, and human psychology is the same. Sometimes they'd be convinced, and sometimes they'd shake their heads and say, 'We'd like to see that evidence.' And I realized they had an excellent point."

Cialdini could have stuck to the laboratory, as he'd been trained to do. He could have built a perfectly successful academic career by devising controlled experiments that—hopefully—mirrored real life. But instead, spurred by his students' questioning, he tried something different.

"I decided to go outside the lab, into the world of influence professionals," he recalls. He wanted to see the world through the eyes of salespeople, marketers, and fundraisers—the people who lived and breathed persuasion. But that was easier said than done. Conducting an experiment outside the confines of academia created complicated new challenges. In an early foray, he decided to test whether it would be possible to increase donations to the United Way in a door-to-door solicitation experiment. "It took us about three times longer to do that study than it would to do any study in the laboratory," he recalls. They needed permission from the police, and to find research assistants willing to knock on strangers' doors and face the possibility of hostile respondents or guard dogs.

Cialdini persisted, and he carefully set up the controls. "We always randomly assigned people," he says. "There was the standard way people normally ask for United Way donations, versus a new and different way, and whether someone got the standard or the new request was randomly assigned based on their house number." For the new version of the request, Cialdini's team added five simple words: "Even a penny would help." The result? Contributions doubled. "How can you say no if even a penny is acceptable?" says Cialdini. "What would you have to think of yourself, to be someone who wouldn't even give a penny? We doubled the number of people who gave, and no one gave a penny, because you don't give a penny to United Way, you give a donation that's appropriate. People don't want to see themselves in a negative light."

Finally, he had an answer for his students' question: he had proven what worked in the real world, not just the laboratory. It's easy to see why others hadn't tried conducting real-world persuasion experiments before; the logistical hassles were substantial. (Notifying the police? Fending off guard dogs?) But Cialdini's decision to try it made all the difference. It propelled him to the heights of his profession: these days, he has a roster of blue-chip consulting clients and is a *New York Times* best-selling author whose work has sold more than two million copies.

The "Big Idea" of bringing influence studies into the field was theoretically available to any psychology researcher.

Cialdini surely wasn't the first professor to be questioned by his students about the lack of real-world data. But he was the one who listened, and who was willing to ask: *Is there a better way?*

Just as Cialdini reshaped psychology, almost any field can be transformed by challenging basic assumptions. Taxis—and their extensive regulation—have been a fact of life in cities for decades. But the rise of smart phones made it possible to ask, *What if you could catch a ride with a regular driver who had spare time on his hands?* Today, ridesharing start-ups like Uber are worth billions of dollars. Spare bedrooms sat empty, until Airbnb created a platform that made short-term rentals easy and appealing, disrupting the hotel industry in the process. And in the past, professionals had to weigh whether their need for administrative help warranted hiring an expensive full-time staffer or locking in a contract with a temporary agency and trusting the luck of the draw. No longer. Online sites like oDesk and Elance allow easy access to short-term administrative help that's been vetted with transparent reviews and recommendations. We're no longer subject to the tyranny of "how things have always been done."

The rewards for challenging the status quo—professional recognition, financial reward, and more—can be substantial, but the path to that happy ending can be winding and dispiriting, so few choose to follow it. Most systems reward those who follow the rules, not those who break them. Professors are praised if they publish frequently in academic journals, and running elaborate experiments that take three times longer than normal is not a good way to get a book out quickly. As we saw with Diane Mulcahy in the introduction, sometimes you get substantial blowback for challenging the underpinnings of an industry; Barry Marshall was treated like a crank because the establishment was convinced, even in the face of medical evidence, that it already knew what caused ulcers. No industry ever welcomes those who challenge its received wisdom, but if you're willing to risk short-term disapprobation, you can ultimately make a substantial contribution to your field. If he hadn't questioned assumptions, Cialdini still could have been a successful professor, but he wouldn't have become a seminal figure who influenced millions. "It seems to me," he says, "the outcome was worth every ounce of inconvenience."

ASK YOURSELF:

- What are others overlooking?
- What are the assumptions underlying your field? Have they been questioned or tested? If so, how long ago—and have circumstances changed in the interim?
- What questions do "newbies" in your field often ask that get shot down or dismissed? Is there a way you could take their questions seriously? What would that look like?
- What's the conventional wisdom about how to do things "the right way" in your field? What if it were actually the opposite? What would that look like?
- What do most people in your field think would be impossible? Is it really? Or is it just difficult?
- What research project or initiative would—if you successfully undertook it—change how your field operates?

WHAT'S NEXT?

Just about everyone can see the really big picture. The Internet is becoming more important every day. Mobile computing will decimate desktops. India's and China's economies are expanding dramatically. Yes . . . and what does any of it mean for us? We know the wave is coming, but how do we make use of that information? How can we prepare to succeed in the new economy? Too many people pontificate about what's happening now, and don't shed any light on the implications moving forward.

If you can find a way to help people prepare for the future—to provide real solutions to upcoming challenges—people will clamor for your practical insights, as Rita Gunther McGrath discovered. A professor at Columbia Business School, she realized the concept of "sustainable competitive advantage" (most famously propounded by the legendary Harvard Business School thinker Michael Porter) had become irrelevant as the pace of change in the corporate world sped up.[2] Years ago, the biggest competitive threats were easy to identify: phone companies only had to worry about other phone companies. Now they need to worry about Apple, which began as a computer company, or Google, which began as a search engine. "The phenomenon [of rapid change] is starting to touch companies that people interact with in their daily lives," such as Nokia and BlackBerry, she says. "It wasn't supposed to be possible that the number-one brand in the world in phones could become irrelevant in five years."

As a result, she began to tackle the question of: *What's next?* When sustainable competitive advantage no longer exists—when other companies can catch up to your product innovations in a year, rather than in a decade—what's your move? McGrath began to develop practical answers for companies wrestling with this question. She suggested speeding up budgeting processes (annually is too slow, so make it quarterly) and creating an ongoing innovation pipeline within the company. Citing the example of Apple, whose massively successful iPhone rendered its own iPod obsolete, she recommended that companies might need to proactively put themselves out of business in certain areas in order to strengthen the company overall. By speaking articulately about the end of competitive advantage and creating a road map for how to succeed in the new business environment, McGrath became a recognized thought leader on the subject. Her hard work paid off: in 2013, she was ranked as the sixth most influential business thinker in the world and won the prestigious Thinkers50 Strategy Award.[3]

It can be tempting—and intellectually easy—to opine about the trends right in front of us. But as McGrath shows, people are hungry for expert guidance as they figure out what these trends mean for their futures. We've all heard the warnings about climate change and increasingly erratic weather patterns. But does that mean we should sell our coastal homes and relocate inland? Or should we stay where we are, but invest in retrofits and reinforcements? Or ignore the warnings and hope for the best? Similarly, we're entering a "flat," geographically agnostic world. How do we best take advantage of that opportunity? By hiring a foreign virtual assistant and outsourcing our work? Relocating to another country and enjoying the lifestyle benefits of "geo-arbitrage"?[4] Buying stock in internationally diversified companies? There's a huge amount of fear and uncertainty about how to respond to our changing circumstances, so if you can provide others with sound, intelligent, actionable advice, your work will be noticed—and appreciated.

So how do you actually know what's next? One secret is staying close to the ground, where research and innovations take place. You can only learn so much by reading newspapers and getting secondhand information. Instead, it's your time in the trenches—talking with those on the front lines and seeing things for yourself—that will help you understand. Robert Scoble, a technology opinion leader, also makes a point of getting firsthand information. "Figure out how to get as close to the research labs as possible," he says. He's become a recognized authority on subjects as diverse as blogging, Google Glass, and Bluetooth low energy radio not because he invented any of them—he didn't—but because he knew their creators, avidly followed the technologies' progress, used them, and wrote and spoke about them. "I'm always looking to meet people who are doing deep research," he says.

Of course, many industries don't have research labs per se, but they all have equivalents—places where new insights are most likely to arise. You may want to track certain think tanks or universities. Maybe the end users or frontline staff in your industry can shed light on emerging trends. Track where the most important advances have come from in the past few years, and you'll understand who you need to be watching to see what's coming. You'll have a particular advantage if, like Robert Scoble, you can find out about emerging developments in the early stages, before they become mainstream. Perhaps you could make a point of attending conferences where new innovations are talked about, reading industry journals, or simply keeping in close touch with colleagues who are "in the know." However you do it, one of the best ways to develop a reputation as an authority in your field is by staying on top of trends, informing others about them, and sharing your take on what they mean and how we should adapt.

ASK YOURSELF:

- What are three trends shaping your industry? Are they short-term or fundamental? How would you describe them to an outsider unfamiliar with your field?
- In the coming years, how will those trends change the status quo?
- What should smart companies or individuals do in order to thrive in the future? How should they prepare? What steps should they take?
- Are there companies or entities that have handled change particularly well? What can you learn from their example?
- What innovations or new developments do you know about that most others do not?
- Where is the locus of innovation in your field? Particular regions or companies or divisions or think tanks? How can you ensure that you stay close to the work they're doing?

WHAT CAN YOU DRAW ON FROM YOUR OWN EXPERIENCE?

To find your Big Idea, you don't need to be a university professor or plugged into the cutting edge of the tech community. It's also possible to draw on your own life and experiences. Some might assume that you can only become "qualified" to offer Big Ideas through formal study—getting a doctorate or spending years working your way up in an industry. Those are great experiences, but not the only ones that matter. Sometimes it's the unexpected elements of your background that create a unique mix that enables you to see things just a bit differently from everyone else. When I interviewed Stuart Crainer—Des Dearlove's partner in the biennial Thinkers50 ranking—for my *Forbes* blog, he told me that they see particularly fresh insights from thinkers with eclectic backgrounds, such as Wharton professor Adam Grant, who worked as a magician; Gianpiero Petriglieri of INSEAD, who is a psychiatrist by training; and celebrated yachtswoman Ellen MacArthur, who gained fame boating solo around the world and has reinvented herself as a business theorist.[5]

For Rose Shuman, it was a jarring personal experience that set her on her life course. When she was eighteen, she took a family trip to visit her stepmom's relatives in Nicaragua. "It was such a jolt to be there, a few years after the Contra War had finished," she says. "It was not in good condition at the time; they had one street signal in the entire country. Growing up in suburban Maryland, it was more than I was equipped to deal with in terms of making sense of things." That trip introduced her to international development, and after college, she made it her career.

She was the director of business development for a UK-based social enterprise that specialized in high-tech eyeglasses aimed at the developing world. More than a billion people worldwide don't have access to an optometrist; Shuman was spending enormous amounts of time in the field, trying to figure out how best to reach them.

One afternoon, she started brainstorming on a related theme: How could you bring the Internet to those same people? We've all heard about the promise of laptops for the poor. But Shuman knew from her travels that this still left many who could likely never take advantage of the technology. "First, they have to learn to read," she says. "Then they need electricity, and to be able to keep their computer in a safe place, and to have an Internet connection. They need to learn to use the computer, and it has to be in a language they know, which there's probably not much of on the Internet—so they'd have to learn a new language. And then they'd have to browse, and maybe something good will happen. That's an enormous number of steps. So how do you collapse and get rid of those steps?"

She spent about four hours hashing out an idea in her notebook, inspired by the public call boxes you might see on a university campus or at a transit station. What if people could connect through a call box with someone who spoke their local language and was sitting in front of a computer, ready to look things up and answer questions? "The last connection would be through voice, so people would never even have to grasp the abstract concept of the Internet," says Shuman. "But you could bring the benefits of it to them right away."

That was the beginning of the Question Box project, a nonprofit initiative now operating in India and sub-Saharan Africa. "It took four hours to conceptualize, and seven years to implement and execute," she says. In the process, she's been named a TED fellow, profiled in *The New York Times*, and lectures at the USC Marshall School of Business.

Users—ranging from students to farmers to orphaned children—ask any question they like, from "Who is the richest man in the world?" to agricultural commodity prices. Shuman's favorite question, she says, was "Did the pyramids ever move?" Fundamentally, she says, the Question Box is a "livelihood enhancement device"—a way to bring the promise of the Internet, and the world's information, to people who would otherwise be shut out.

On one hand, Shuman's story appears to be the ultimate, Archimedes-like flash of "Big Idea" inspiration. In one electrifying four-hour brainstorming session, she mapped out a vision for her life's work. But she couldn't have developed the idea without the inspiration of her teenage family trip to Nicaragua, or the intensive on-the-ground research she'd done in developing countries. And the idea, great though it was, wasn't sufficient on its own. It's required nearly a decade of subsequent work to implement it around the world.

Outsiders often wonder at Big Ideas: *It must have taken a genius to have come up with something like that!* Of course, the thought leaders profiled are all smart people, but developing a Big Idea doesn't require genius. What's required are skills that many professionals already have—the ability to ask good questions, to challenge assumptions, and to listen to your gut instinct that alerts you when the rest of the world is overlooking something. Ultimately, it requires hard work and patience, as you work to spread and actualize your Big Idea.

In *Where Good Ideas Come From*, Steven Johnson talks about the power of the "slow hunch." Some of the best ideas take time, even years, to percolate. Charles Darwin, for instance, posited rough versions of the theory of evolution in his journal for months before it finally coalesced in his mind. For many of us, our Big Idea is an iterative process—refining a concept, or answering new questions that arise in the course of our work. Because of your unique experiences, you already see things differently from anyone else. Pay attention to what's in front of you—whether it's a call box or the beak of a finch—and let it suggest new ideas and directions for your work. If you really look, and really listen, you can see things in a new way.

ASK YOURSELF:

- What personal experience have you had that's changed your view of the world?
- Think about the jobs you've held, the projects you've worked on, or the body of work you've created. What question logically arises from the ones you've tackled before?
- What experiences have you had that others in your field most likely have not? How does that difference shape your view of the industry?

Develop Your Expert Niche

I n thought leadership, sometimes you succeed by going big—Robert Cialdini cracking the code of influence and persuasion, or Rita McGrath explaining how businesses can thrive amid the end of competitive advantage. But other times, depending on your passions and goals, it's better to narrowcast. Instead of developing a broad theory about how the world works or the direction of the future, you can become the go-to authority on a particular slice that has been overlooked, an area where your extensive knowledge, and ability to communicate it, shines. Once you've established yourself there, you can often expand your influence to other realms.

Building a base of knowledge in a narrow subject area may seem like a career-limiting move, but sometimes it's the only way to get past the competition. If your field already contains multiple thought leaders, it will be hard for you to gain recognition. Readers will trust the established experts and have no reason to turn to you—unless your expertise in a subsection of the field surpasses that of the general experts.

Take the world of technology. "If you want to be known as a tech blogger, you're competing with *TechCrunch*, and *Gigaom*, and *The Verge*," says Robert Scoble. "That's almost 150 people at three blogs. Are you really going to be able to rise above the noise level, with one person? I don't think so."

Fortunately, there's a solution. Scoble suggests choosing one segment to specialize in so that your coverage can be much deeper than that of even the better-funded establishment players. *TechCrunch* may cover nanotechnology, for instance, but if you write exclusively about that subject, you're going to rapidly outstrip them and become the definitive source on the subject. In this chapter, we'll cover how to find the niche you want to own, distinguish yourself from others in the field, develop your skills so you're regarded as an unparalleled authority, and, finally, how to expand your reputation so you're ultimately able to move far beyond your initial specialty.

FINDING YOUR NICHE

The first step is finding your niche. What are you qualified—and sufficiently interested in—to talk about? Perhaps it's a hobby you've been pursuing since childhood. Maybe you've been researching one topic for years, or have an advanced degree in a particular subject. It could be the result of extensive personal study, as was the case with Ramit Sethi, creator of the popular blog (and later *New York Times* bestseller) *I Will Teach You to Be Rich*. He wasn't a CPA or financial planner. Instead, he learned about personal finance in the trenches. "We didn't have a lot of money and my parents said, 'If you want to go to college, you have to get scholarships,'" he told me. "And so I built a system to apply to about sixty-five or seventy of them, and I ended up paying my way through college." That was a win—but he learned even more from an early loss. He decided to invest his first scholarship check in the stock market, hoping to grow its value. He lost half of it. "I was like, 'Oh, I better learn how money works,'" he recalls, which led him to his new career. Sometimes, in situations like this, the path is obvious.

But what if you're not sure where to start? A good first step is to follow your passions and see where they lead. For four years, Nate Silver was a bored accounting firm employee. He tried to entertain himself with a mix of activities blending the Internet, statistics, and ratings—first, by creating a Web site called Burrito Bracket that rated Mexican restaurants in Chicago, and then by playing Internet poker.[1] He'd picked up basic statistics in college as an economics major. And in his spare time, like many Americans, he followed baseball. But instead of simply watching games and rooting for his favorite team, he decided to create a tool for ranking players' performance—one that turned out to be remarkably accurate.

After it was acquired by the Web site Baseball Prospectus, Silver managed the system for several years until his interest was piqued by another complex and misunderstood phenomenon he loved: politics. Pollsters released innumerable public opinion surveys, but their findings were all over the map. Was there a way, he wondered, to make better predictions? During the 2008 campaign season, he created the *FiveThirtyEight* blog to answer the question, wielding statistical analysis in a far more sophisticated way than most reporters. (The name refers to the number of votes in the electoral college.) In the process, Nate Silver built a devoted following and called the election with stunning accuracy.

When Silver ran into the editor of *The New York Times Magazine* on an Amtrak platform in Boston in the spring of 2010, a deal was struck. At first, he agreed to contribute a few pieces to the magazine. But soon, the courtship bloomed, and the *Times* licensed his blog for a three-year period, through the 2012 elections (which Silver predicted perfectly).[2] He wrote a best-selling book and built a massive fan base. The day before the election, his blog accounted for 20 percent of *The New York Times*'s entire online traffic. In 2013, he moved *FiveThirtyEight* to ESPN, where he presided over a newsroom of sports, politics, and economics reporters—all immersed in his statistics-driven approach to news coverage.

Silver wasn't a professional statistician; he doesn't even have a master's degree. But, thanks to his college studies, he knew *enough*. He didn't know right away that he wanted to transform baseball or politics. He experimented first with burritos and poker. But he followed his passions and eventually found ways to apply his expertise in unusual places where it was truly valued. Baseball and politics are vastly different. But Silver's ability to translate complex numbers into a meaningful narrative transcended those boundaries and made him a household name.

FOCUSING YOUR NICHE

You may find that you have so many passions, it's hard to focus on one. That was the problem I faced a number of years ago. I'd been working as a self-employed marketing consultant, and wanted to write a book—both to fulfill a long-standing personal goal, and also as a means of attracting new business. But the question of what to write about was tricky. In my consulting work, I was a generalist. I helped clients create marketing plans and social media strategies, not to mention working with them on messaging and media relations. I used to work as a presidential campaign spokesperson and as a journalist, plus I'd run a nonprofit, directed a documentary film, and had been a theology student. It was hard to figure out what facet of my experience I should write about, and—critically—what would actually interest other people.

It was only when I started blogging for *Harvard Business Review* in 2010 that my focus clarified. The second post I ever wrote for them was called "How to Reinvent Your Personal Brand"—a topic that interested me because of my numerous career changes. It wasn't necessarily meant to be my definitive statement to the world; it was one seven-hundred-word blog post, out of dozens I'd done before, and hundreds I'd do subsequently. But for some reason, this one caught on. It received tons of comments on the Web site, and the editors asked me to write an expanded version for the *Harvard Business Review* magazine. Within a week of its publication, three different literary agents had reached out to me, asking if I'd be interested in representation. Two years later, my book *Reinventing You* was released, and I've subsequently lectured around the world about personal branding and professional reinvention.

Sometimes you have to experiment with a lot of ideas and see which one sticks. If you're unsure, let the market decide. Which posts receive the most comments, or retweets, or e-mail inquiries? What seems to capture people's imagination? Finding your niche is not an exact science, and you often won't know in advance what will work. If I had waited for the right idea, I'd probably still be waiting. Instead, I tried out a variety and, in the process, learned which one people cared about.

CREATING YOUR NICHE

My challenge was having too many ideas to pursue, but some people have the opposite problem, and worry they don't have *any* areas of expertise. If that's you, don't be too sure. Expertise takes many forms, and almost anyone can become an expert at something, if they're strategic about how and where they can add value. You don't have to be the number-one expert in your field; context matters. It's not necessary to be Shakespeare to be known around the office as a good writer, and you don't need to be Arnold Schwarzenegger to be a successful fitness coach.

Michael Leckie, a regional vice president at the research firm Gartner, developed a reputation in his company for being an expert on coaching and talent development, even though—by his own admission—he certainly didn't start out as one. Compared with worldwide authorities, he was a novice, but he knew more than others at the firm, put in the effort to expand his knowledge, and was willing to share what he learned. "When you start building your brand in a corporation, it's a confined space," he says. "You don't need to be the best in the world; you just need to be the best one there. You can be a big fish in a little pond, and if you're the biggest fish in that environment, you get bigger and can then start to do things outside the organization." That's enabled him to propel his career forward.

Similarly, if you're a reasonably good writer, you could start coaching your colleagues (with their permission, of course) on how to write better business memos or e-mails. If you're interested in health, you could lead a running group, which may generate client leads for a new fitness coaching business. If you're passionate about mindfulness, you could start a class at your office (that worked for Chade-Meng Tan, a Google engineer whose "Search Inside Yourself" classes at the Googleplex led to international recognition and a book deal).

Finally, how do you avoid choosing a niche that's *too* narrow? Ask yourself whether your subject has enough material to stay interesting over time. That strategy worked well for Brian Stelter, a young journalist whose detailed blog covering the television news industry caught the attention of *The New York Times*, which eventually hired him (he later moved on to CNN). He chose a subject narrow enough that he could cover it far better than the mainstream media, which would write about it only if something major happened, but also broad enough that there's always material (which wouldn't be the case if his blog was entirely devoted to one newscaster).

Many people hesitate to "niche down." The overly modest are concerned that they're not *really* experts, and the renaissance people don't want to feel trapped. But remember: Finding and embracing a niche can be powerful because, first, as long as you know more than the people around you, you're making a real contribution. And second, as we'll discuss later in the chapter, developing one niche is often the fastest ticket to expanding into adjacent areas. For now, let's turn to a critical element that aspiring thinkers can't afford to overlook: distinguishing yourself in your niche.

ASK YOURSELF:

- What are the topics you feel passionate about (even if they don't seem like clear professional money-makers)?
- What topics are you a "local expert" in—that is, not necessarily the best in the world, but better or more knowledgeable than those around you?
- Have other people built careers around any of the above topics—and if so, how? (Homemaking and baking didn't seem nearly so lucrative until Martha Stewart made her mark.)

DISTINGUISHING YOURSELF IN YOUR NICHE

If you're specializing in an emerging area like nanotechnology, staking out new turf isn't that hard. No one has written about your topic extensively before, and with enough effort, you can become the leading authority. But what about areas that are more well trod? How can you distinguish yourself enough to get noticed? That was the problem facing Rachael Ray, and as her example shows, it's often a matter of reframing your expertise so that what's banal in one setting becomes revelatory in another.

In her world—the world of cooking—it's pretty clear what "expert" means: you run a high-end restaurant, or you've been trained at elite cooking schools. Rachael Ray did neither. She started out as the food buyer for a gourmet market in Albany, New York, and began doing "thirty-minute meal" cooking demonstrations at the store to showcase ingredients.[3] The store didn't choose her for the role because of her prodigious talents; it was because no chef in the area would accept the store's low rates. When her boss was fired, she quit out of loyalty and landed another job doing cooking demos around the region for the Price Chopper grocery store chain.

Her traveling demonstrations eventually led to a weekly cooking show on a local Albany TV station, and in 1999, she wrote her first cookbook (published by a tiny, one-woman press). The story could have ended there, but in 2001, Ray had a stroke of luck: a *Today* show producer had been given her cookbook as a gift. When a snowstorm brought a rash of guest cancellations, the producer decided to give Ray a try. Ray drove nine hours through the snow to make it into New York City. She aced the show and the next morning, the Food Network offered her a $360,000 contract, launching her career. It's a fairy-tale story so incredible, she became a Harvard Business School case study.[4] But *why* was she chosen?

Compared with Emeril Lagasse or Mario Batali, decorated chefs and James Beard award winners, her credentials were woefully insufficient. As she recalled in a *Vanity Fair* interview, "I said, 'Listen, you're champagne, I'm beer out of the bottle. I clearly don't belong here. I'm not a chef, you've been duped.' And I got up."[5] But the Food Network executives were looking for something different. "They said, 'No, no, no, stop. That's what we like. We don't want you to be a chef.'"

We don't want you to be a chef. Those are bizarre words coming from the leaders of a network dedicated to food, but they're telling. By the traditional standards of expertise, Ray is—as she freely admits—"grossly under-qualified."[6] But she's an expert in something different, not high-end French cuisine or molecular gastronomy, but the art of making food easy and accessible to regular people. Some wouldn't even call that expertise; plenty of people complain that their mom/wife/friend can cook as well as Rachael Ray can, so why is she on TV? But that's missing the point.

If Rachael Ray were just another neighbor on your block, her ability to make tasty thirty-minute meals would be nice, but not earth-shattering. But in the context of the Food Network—which had built a brand around celebrity chefs like Emeril Lagasse—she was a revelation. They needed someone whose spunky, regular-gal charm could offset the potentially alienating expertise of someone who had been named the best restaurateur in America. Lagasse may be great to watch, but viewers could rightly ask: Can I even hope for my meals to turn out like his? With Rachael Ray, they didn't have to wonder.

Your expertise doesn't have to include the most prestigious diplomas or accolades; sometimes you just have to know how to do something different in a given context, and do it well. Think about who needs your skills or approach, but doesn't typically have access to them. There are plenty of people who speak Spanish in the world, but if you're the only bilingual financial planner in your office, that gives you a competitive advantage and makes you the go-to person for an entire group of potential customers. If you have great communication skills and work at a software company, you could be an invaluable bridge between engineers (who often struggle to avoid tech jargon) and customers. If you're a corporate executive with a passion for environmental issues, you may be uniquely valuable to the cause because of your knowledge of how the business world operates and how to influence corporate policy.

Becoming recognized in your niche is a pitched battle when you're up against others who have the exact same credentials you do. If they have better connections or even just a sliver more talent, your chances are slim. If you change the context and compete in a space where you're unique, as

Rachael Ray did, you may find yourself a hot commodity. You're injecting fresh ideas and energy into the discussion; you're offering something genuinely different, and that gives you a competitive advantage.

ASK YOURSELF:

- Is there a way you can differentiate yourself from others in your profession?
- What is the traditional background of influential players in your field? Is there a way to leverage being the opposite of that?
- Is there a realm you're interested in where your skill set is rare or hasn't been fully utilized in the past?
- What weakness can become your strength? Is there an area where you *don't have* credentials or expertise, and could that become a selling point?

DEVELOPING YOUR NICHE

At this point, you've identified your niche and determined how to distinguish yourself in the marketplace. Now you need to develop your niche so that you're moving from *an* expert to *the* expert—taking your knowledge to the next level, and creating an insurmountable barrier between you and the competition. You can do this through formal study, but it's not strictly necessary. In fact, one of the best ways to develop your niche is through creating your own personal curriculum. Identify the skills you'd like to learn, and think through how you can best obtain them. Sometimes it's a paid degree program, but it could also be through à la carte classes at local adult education centers or university extension schools. You could do an internship or part-time apprenticeship with someone you admire. You could identify free information sources you like and binge on them. On my Web site, I've compiled more than four hundred free articles that I've written for sites such as *Forbes* and *Harvard Business Review,* covering marketing, branding, message development, leadership, personal branding, and more. Many authors offer similar archives. Personally, one of my goals this past year was to learn more about online marketing, so I've made a point of listening regularly to a number of excellent free podcasts like *Smart Passive Income, EntrepreneurOnFire,* and more. Once you find sites or podcasts you enjoy, you can listen almost endlessly; as of this writing, *EntrepreneurOnFire* alone has well over three hundred hours of free audio content.

If you'd prefer a structured course, you could learn online via a MOOC—or make your own reading list. Josh Kaufman essentially earned his own "degree" by reading the top business books on his own. He chronicled his efforts in the popular book *The Personal MBA.* You could do the same with your chosen field, and in the process become vastly more knowledgeable than most people who simply read what others tell them to or assume they'll pick up what they need to know by osmosis.

Finally, you can learn simply through doing. "I think the best training is almost always going to be hands-on training," Nate Silver told *Harvard Business Review.*[7] "Getting your hands dirty with the data set is, I think, far and away better than spending too much time doing reading and so forth." He didn't start out as an expert statistician; he knew just enough to get started, and in the process of mucking around with burrito rankings, he became an expert. If you're curious and willing to work hard, you can teach yourself what you need to develop your niche and get to the next level.

ASK YOURSELF:

- What topics within your niche do you want to learn more about?
- What books, Web sites, or podcasts can teach you the most about them?
- How can you test out your ideas in low-risk ways (conduct a survey before creating a product, write a blog post before penning an entire book, conduct an informational interview with someone who has previously done what you want to do, etc.)?

EXPANDING YOUR NICHE

Finally, it's time to expand your niche. Once you've become a recognized expert in one area, it's infinitely easier to move into new realms. One reason is a phenomenon in psychology known as the "halo effect," in which—because you're already perceived as good at one thing—people generalize and think you're brilliant overall. That means if you're the authority on Google Glass, you're likely to be called for comment about Google's self-driving cars. (It's important to be honest about the limits of your expertise here: some people might actually buy a brand of toothpaste if Dr. Phil recommended it, but he probably shouldn't make the endorsement unless he's been moonlighting in dental school.) Second, in a very tactical sense, the connections you make through your initial expertise can help you as you diversify. (If you've written an op-ed for a newspaper on a given topic, the editor—who now knows you and your writing style—may be more receptive to your pitch on a different theme.)

One master of niche expansion is Sophal Ear. When he was a baby, his mother fled the Khmer Rouge, the genocidal rulers of Cambodia, and saved her five children. Nearly thirty years later, when he grew up and began studying for his Ph.D. in political economy at the University of California at Berkeley, he wondered about the homeland he'd fled and decided to study it. "It fuels those late nights, that drive to do as much as possible because I feel a sense of responsibility," he says. "I've been fortunate: I got out of Cambodia alive."

On the surface, choosing to become an expert on Cambodia might not look like a good career move for an aspiring academic. Scholars are evaluated on how many times their work is cited, and compared with the intense geopolitical interest in China or India, Cambodia is an afterthought in the academic world. Ear recognized that concentrating his studies on Cambodia decreased his chances of recognition, but he wasn't deterred: "I'd rather do what I'm passionate about."

His dissertation focused on foreign aid in Cambodia. That deep dive into a narrow topic allowed him to accelerate his mastery of the field, and when opportunities to pivot came along, he took them. His dissertation chair took on a project with the UN agricultural commission and needed someone to write a paper on livestock in Cambodia; Ear agreed to do it as long as it could fit in with his dissertation.

You never know where your breaks will come from: when the avian flu broke out, Ear's knowledge of Asian livestock made him a sought-after expert. Indeed, it turned out that his specialty could serve as an entry point into many topics. "I'm not the kind of professor who stays in my lane when it comes to research," he says. "One door is Cambodia and it leads to all kinds of possibilities." He's even given a popular TED talk about criminal tribunals and justice, stemming from his family's experience with the Khmer Rouge.

Despite his focus on a country that doesn't get much press, Ear has found a way to extend his expertise into the most disparate realms imaginable. He recently became a tenured professor at Occidental College, and emphatically plans to keep his research focused outside the ivory tower: "I'm going to write and . . . it's not to create ideas that are going to be collecting dust on a bookshelf, but to have an impact on the world."

If you're strategic, like Ear, you can leverage your niche expertise into a broader role as a thought leader. The secret is thinking through *related* areas where you can add value. He wasn't moving from Cambodian politics into football or ballet or Hollywood movies. Instead, he leveraged his core knowledge and expanded steadily into adjacent fields, where the connection made sense. Over time, as his expertise and reputation in those areas grow, he can move farther afield. (For instance, an expertise in Cambodia leads to an expertise in avian flu, which—if he pursues it—could lead to an expertise in the spread of other infectious diseases that have nothing to do with Cambodia.) Once you've gotten a toehold, you can rapidly expand your brand and the realms in which you're considered an expert.

ASK YOURSELF:

- Once you've established your expertise in a niche, what are the adjacent areas you could move into?

- How can you begin to solidify your credentials in the new areas (writing blog posts or op-eds, giving speeches, serving on committees related to those disciplines, etc.)?

- What are upcoming news events that will make your expertise relevant? (For Ear, the trial of Khmer Rouge leaders might trigger media interest in his work on criminal justice, for instance.)

- How can you capitalize on those moments (reaching out to existing media contacts, etc.)?

Provide
New
Research

3

I n a world of uncertainty and over-the-top punditry, where everyone has an opinion (and shares it relentlessly in the blogosphere), people are hungry for actual data. Small businesses want to know if their marketing is truly generating ROI. Investors wonder if the CEO is a brilliant strategist or the beneficiary of a bull market. Prospective home buyers wonder how to tell if purchasing that house is a good idea. If you're able to offer data that is new, accurate, and revealing, you're very quickly going to become a sought-after source.

Many people shy away from creating new research because they assume it has to be expensive and inordinately time-consuming. It's true that you're never going to match the research clout of corporations with deep pockets and full-time staff; while it would be illuminating for you to conduct a nationwide phone survey of 100,000 people, it's probably not going to happen. But if you're willing to put in the time and effort, there are other, less expensive ways to unearth data or create a fact-based analysis that will enliven the public discourse. All it takes is a desire to seek out information and present it in a fresh way, along with a willingness to work hard.

Sometimes it's reviews that set you apart—taking the time to analyze a complex subject thoughtfully and knowledgeably—or other forms of on-the-ground research. When you immerse yourself in the daily reality of a situation and speak directly to those on the front lines, you get a nuanced perspective that isn't accessible to casual observers. Whatever form of research you choose, it's essential to ensure that it reaches as many people as possible and is worth your investment of time and money. In this chapter, we'll discuss how to conduct small-scale but valuable research and to make sure your hard work gets in front of the people who need to see it.

THE POWER OF RESEARCH

It was the turn of the millennium, and Michael Waxenberg—an IT director for a financial services firm—and his wife were living in a crumbling rental building on New York City's Upper West Side. They'd just had a baby and started to wonder: do we really want to raise a family here? They went to open houses, but prices were high, so they decided to wait. But by 2005, real estate matters had become more pressing. Their landlord had sold the building and the new owners began converting it from rentals into condominiums. They had to decide soon: buy or move?

Waxenberg discovered the Web site StreetEasy, which featured a discussion board where readers would sometimes post brief reviews of properties. He decided to join in, sharing his thoughts from the open houses. Taking reviews to a new level, he wrote thoughtful and detailed reports on his specialty: multibedroom, prewar Upper West Side apartments like the one his family was living in. "I gradually became the go-to guy for that micromarket," he says. "I was the guy who knew what to look for in a ninety-year-old apartment, what kind of floor plans converted well to three and four bedrooms, and which buildings were friendly to which kinds of renovations. I built a dialogue with various real estate agents, and by tapping their knowledge, I got a little more of an insider's perspective on buildings."

He was proud of his qualitative reviews, but felt they weren't sufficient on their own. Site readers would comment on the pricing of various units, but Waxenberg felt it was "very unstructured, very anecdotal, and . . . had no real statistical validity. Because I'm a data guy, that stuck in my craw a little bit." So in late 2007, he started a discussion thread focused strictly on the numbers, asking contributors to share hard data on sale prices. It became so large and so popular, it quickly split from a citywide discussion strand into separate ones for each neighborhood. He participated actively in the Upper West Side discussion, which soon grew to more than two thousand posts.

Fellow StreetEasy readers began reaching out for his expert opinion: Would he serve as their Realtor? There was only one problem: he didn't have a license. He said he was happy to offer advice, but couldn't actually represent them. "I got cases of wine and boxes of chocolates, but I couldn't collect commissions," he says. Eventually, though, he caught the notice of an actual Realtor. In late 2008, established real estate agent Keith Burkhardt, intrigued by Waxenberg's thoughtful commentary, e-mailed him an offer: *If you're not already a Realtor, I'll sponsor you.*

Waxenberg was originally skeptical; he felt that most Manhattan Realtors were part of "a giant conspiracy to drive prices up" in a heated market. "I have a tenant's perspective," says Waxenberg. "The middle class is being squeezed out of New York, and it very nearly happened to us." Overcoming Waxenberg's suspicions, Burkhardt, who runs an innovative full-service brokerage at discount prices, won him over. Intrigued by the possibility of putting his knowledge to work to help families like his find homes, Waxenberg took the requisite courses and got his license.

He'd built his brand so successfully, he landed business immediately from fellow StreetEasy readers, and his clientele today is made up of their second-generation referrals. He still works full-time in IT; for him, real estate is "a relatively lucrative hobby." But most important, in July 2011—more than a decade after he immersed himself in Upper West Side open houses—his family finally bought their home.

Everyone loves to opine about real estate, and what's overpriced and what isn't. But Waxenberg made a contribution—and got noticed for it—because he was committed to injecting *fact* into the conversation. He visited more than one thousand apartments on the Upper West Side, acquiring a tremendous knowledge base. And he didn't keep that information to himself; he shared it through his own reviews, and encouraged others to pool their collective knowledge via the discussion thread on verified sale prices. As his example shows, when you put in the time to gain knowledge and share it, you'll be recognized for it. Michael Waxenberg didn't set out to become a real estate agent, but the path opened itself up because of his efforts. When you put in the work, clients and opportunities will come to you—a situation any professional would relish.

Depending on your field, conducting research and writing reviews can be one of the fastest—and cheapest—ways to become a trusted source. Reviewing rarely requires a graduate degree or special licensing. Instead, it takes a willingness to spend time, a genuine interest in the field, and a desire to help others make the best decisions possible.

Waxenberg started as an amateur real estate enthusiast; Nate Silver got his start handicapping burritos. You can review anything, from beer to business books to online courses to hotels to opera performances to cars. The best reviews are extremely detailed, setting them apart from the lackluster effort that most volunteer reviewers put forward, and display enough familiarity with the field to easily show how a given product differs from its competitors. They also understand the hot-button issues that customers will care about, drawn from personal passion and experience, as well as conversations with other interested consumers.

You could do write-ups on your own blog or (if you're less concerned about building up your own site traffic) via established sites like TripAdvisor. In fact, reviews can become big business. I first ran across a young woman named Robin Liss, then a college student, more than a decade ago when she went to work for an opposing presidential candidate. In her spare time, she was an entrepreneur running product review sites for everything from camcorders to ovens to laundry machines. In 2011, at age twenty-six, she sold her group of review sites (by then, she covered twelve product categories) to *USA Today*.[1] Most people who are shopping for a product or service won't have the interest or ability to dig that deep. So when they discover that you've done the work for them, they'll likely be grateful for your efforts and quick to recognize your superior expertise. That's a fast path to becoming a recognized authority.

ASK YOURSELF:

- What area or question do you feel passionate about researching?
- Think about what research your field could benefit from. What do you—and others—wish you knew?
- How could you find that out? Think broadly; it could involve field research, case studies, interviews, focus groups, number crunching, or other methods.
- Are there products, services, or businesses that aren't being reviewed sufficiently (or at all)? What would you do differently?

- Is there an existing place where you could contribute your knowledge? If not, could you create a venue where people can collect and share information?

FIND THE HIDDEN STORY

Waxenberg distinguished himself with in-depth reviews, drawn from his thousand-plus visits to Upper West Side open houses. A crucial element of his success was a willingness to go into the trenches and conduct on-the-ground research. He wasn't sitting at home clicking on YouTube videos that Realtors had posted; he was visiting the houses himself, and writing up thoughtful, honest assessments. Legendary business consultants Tom Peters and Bob Waterman showed a similar desire to roll up their sleeves and get answers for themselves. In their case, they weren't working on reviews. Their mission was to seek out hidden stories— the ones that weren't being told.

Read enough business literature and you'll see the same faces, again and again. In the late 1970s, when they were conducting their research, and even today, it's a hit list of the usual CEO suspects, pontificating about why they're so successful. That's why Peters and Waterman decided to focus their research—which resulted in the 1982 blockbuster book *In Search of Excellence*—on the stories that weren't being told in the business world.

Today, the idea of profiling exemplary American businesses may seem banal. But in the late 1970s and early 1980s, the United States was enmeshed not just in a recession, but in a crisis of confidence. Japanese cars were trouncing their American competitors; Japan's economy was growing at a blistering rate. The popular narrative at the time was that America had stagnated, and in order to be effective, you had to learn to think, and manage, like the Japanese. Few thought researching American companies was worthwhile.

Peters and Waterman didn't set out to create a patriotic narrative. "Bob and I weren't flag wavers," says Peters. But they did tell a story others weren't, identifying American companies that—in the midst of recession and competitive threats—were nonetheless succeeding. "It seemed like almost every management book was about bad news and how to fix it," says Peters. "And ours was about good news, period."

When your message is different—not for the sake of being different, but because your research has uncovered an overlooked story—you're likely to draw attention. Peters certainly did, selling more than two million copies of his book and becoming one of the most prominent business gurus of the 1980s.

Besides focusing their research on American companies, Peters and Waterman also asked questions of people often ignored by researchers, who sought to interview CEOs. Peters figured that a C-level perspective would be so high level, it wouldn't necessarily shed light on management in the trenches. "Our perfect person was a division general manager," he says, explaining that these managers were close enough to the action that they wouldn't just wax philosophical about best practices. Instead, they'd be able to share stories about what they actually did on a day-to-day basis. As Peters told me when I interviewed him at his Vermont home, "Everybody likes a good story." Drawing on information gleaned from lower-level employees, Peters was able to create compelling case studies, something not common at the time.

When they did talk to top leaders, Peters and Waterman deliberately spoke to heads of companies that weren't attracting the attention of the business community. Peters recalls Hewlett-Packard in the late 1970s as being "kind of cool, but not particularly high visibility" when compared with the stalwarts that were often profiled in business books. When he reached out to the company, he not only got to tell a fresh story, he also got unprecedented access to the company's decision makers. "I said to the receptionist at HP, 'I'd really like to talk to John Young [the president], if I could,' and thirty-five seconds later, I'm talking to John Young. Now, if you'd been working with the Chases or Citibanks . . . there would be three or four levels" before you'd be permitted to talk with them.

Looking in unusual places had its benefits. When Peters visited HP headquarters, he was shocked by their approach. He wasn't given a visitors' badge that limited his access; he could explore at will. And he learned that Young shared an eight-by-eight cubicle with his secretary—an egalitarian ethos common today, but unheard of in the late 1970s. John Young clearly did things differently from the CEOs everyone else was profiling.

"We're sitting talking with John, and he introduces us to the idea of 'managing by wandering around,'" Peters recalls. "And it's been the keystone to everything I've done since." Popularized by Peters, Young's idea became a catch-phrase and an obsession for a generation of leaders. And Peters and Waterman wouldn't have discovered it if they'd stuck to the script and written a traditional business book talking to traditional CEOs.

To have the greatest effect in your research, go against the current. Look for the stories no one else is telling—or the ones that haven't been discovered yet. As McKinsey consultants with access at the highest levels, it would have been easy for Peters and Waterman to content themselves with visiting the pooh-bahs of industry and recording their thoughts for posterity. That also would have made for a boring, disconnected, and self-congratulatory book. Instead, they searched for the outliers—the companies like HP that were doing something different and unconventional. If everyone is talking about hot start-ups, what lessons can you extract from established companies that have managed to stay successful for the past century? If business magazines are lionizing CEOs, what could you learn by talking to COOs about the nitty-gritty of how the business really operates? If everyone's looking to Asia as the market of the future, what can you unearth by focusing on South America or Africa? By discovering hidden gems and spreading those ideas (like Peters and the "management by wandering around" concept), you can make a mark.

ASK YOURSELF:

- Who are the usual information sources in your industry? Who else is knowledgeable, but doesn't often get asked for their insights or opinions? How can you reach out to them?

- What on-the-ground field research can you conduct in your area of interest? Who can you visit or interview about their experiences?
- Is there a hidden "good news story" in your field that most others aren't aware of or talking about?

LEVERAGING YOUR RESEARCH INVESTMENT

Peters, backed by McKinsey, had the resources to research *In Search of Excellence* full-time. But most of us have many other competing obligations; we don't have time and money to spare. So how can you make your research count so that it justifies the effort? The secret is getting your research process to do double duty. Done right, research can both educate you about a given industry and put you in contact with the most influential people in it. That way, it's an investment in professional development *and* network building, so you can afford to spend more time on it.

The marketing of your research should also serve your professional interests. Before the research is complete, think through your plan for content creation. As the social media strategist Gary Vaynerchuk told me, "It's not good enough to just produce long-form content; you have to put out microcontent to drive awareness to it." He might write a blog post about a given topic, and also create a video and an animated GIF about that same topic. If you really wanted to maximize your effort and attract more viewers, you could also create tweets promoting your blog, video, and gif; Facebook posts; an audio file; a short video on Vine to complement a longer one on YouTube or Vimeo; and the list goes on. If you're going to take the time to create something, you owe it to yourself to make it amazing—and ensure that the right people see your work.

Mark Fidelman, a San Diego–based entrepreneur and consultant, has mastered the process. He's an avid blogger for sites like *Forbes* and *Business Insider.* But he's not doing it for the pay (little) or even the vague promise of "exposure." Instead, he writes his heavily researched posts for two reasons: "Either I have a new client and I need to get up to speed on their business, and writing forces me to be intelligent about it," he says, "or I'll use it for lead generation, in hopes that people connect with me and want to hire my company or join my network."

When Fidelman takes on a client, he doesn't write about them directly. Instead, he interviews leaders who work in his client's industry and uses the interview process as a form of networking. One of his strategies is to create elaborately researched posts that identify the top twenty-five leaders in a given field or industry ("The 25 Highest Rated CEOs That Are Hiring Now," or "Meet the Top 20 Most Social CMOs of the Fortune 100," or "The World's Top 20 Social Brands"). Creating each list, he says, takes at least one hundred hours. That may seem like a mammoth undertaking, but he's convinced of the value: It gives him the opportunity to build relationships with influential people who might be useful connections for him and his clients in the future. Plus, he's developed a precise system to leverage his time.

He starts with four hundred to five hundred names of possible contenders and narrows them down on a first pass by their Klout score, which measures their online influence. (He hires two freelancers from online sites such as oDesk or Elance, at a cost of $5 to $6 per hour, to check and recheck the scoring.) That'll reduce the list to a more manageable one hundred, at which point he evaluates whether each potential influencer talks about the subject in question (such as crowdfunding) more than 50 percent of the time. If not, he eliminates them from contention.

Then, he and his contractors cross-reference other social metrics—their Kred scores, Alexa rankings, how popular their blog is, how often they're retweeted, how often they're quoted or mentioned in Google search results, and more. Fidelman is aiming for seven or eight data points, which he turns into a weighted average. Then he narrows the list to twenty-five, and runs a final check to make sure the finalists haven't gamed the system by purchasing fake Twitter followers. His last step is a spot check with industry insiders: "Do these top five sound right or not?"

Once the list is solidified, Fidelman ensures the effort won't go to waste. He uses a graphic designer in Eastern Europe, who charges only $10 an hour, to turn the influencer list into an infographic. "I try to make my content shareable as much as possible," he says. "I might create a SlideShare about it. I think, how do I repurpose this information so it spreads far and wide?" He'll even follow up by asking each influencer for one tip about succeeding in their field, and will put them into an e-book. He sets up a landing page for the e-book and requests the e-mail address of people who'd like to download it. "That gets leads for my client," he says, "and most of the top twenty-five are helping me promote it because they're in it." He's managed to leverage the most powerful people in an industry to generate leads for his client.

Spending one hundred hours to create one blog post sounds like madness, but it's a winning formula for Fidelman. "The whole reason is to pay it forward to these influencers," he says. "If I recognize them in a big way, they'll repay me or my client fivefold. I develop pretty strong relationships with ninety percent of them. If I know the most influential people in an industry, it makes me more valuable to my clients."

The whole process is a carefully constructed win-win. Fidelman provides interesting research to the public (most readers are quite interested in who the top players are in a given industry, as evinced by the hundreds of thousands of views his posts have generated). He gives public recognition to thoughtful professionals who are at the top of their field. And in the process, he educates himself about various industries and builds personal connections that may be valuable to his clients or prospective clients. These days, we're all busy. No one has a spare hour, much less a spare hundred, to conduct research. But Fidelman shows how you can integrate research into your professional life and make it an integral part of how you do business.

■ How can you make sure your research accomplishes multiple goals (as with Fidelman's use of writing for professional development and lead generation)?

■ Can you create a system to leverage your time investment (getting help with certain areas of the research, writing, or publicity process)?

■ How can you spread the results of your research even more widely? Are there ways to create spin-off content (e-books, infographics, SlideShares, etc.) from the original research?

Combine
Ideas

4

You might imagine that your passion for fantasy football, or your master's degree in Italian literature, or your skill in juggling would be pretty irrelevant to your future success. (After all, who would've thought that Steve Jobs's college class in calligraphy would result in a worldwide impact on design and aesthetics?) But those skills may actually provide the perspective you need to understand the world just differently enough to make a contribution. Some of the most significant ideas come about when someone sees a problem in a new way—often by combining disparate elements that initially seemed unrelated. That's where your unique gifts come into play; no one has the exact same training and background as you do, so no one else can see a problem exactly the way you do. Bringing your whole self to the challenge—everything you've done and learned before—is what will allow you to combine ideas into exciting new forms.

Harvard Medical School professor Albert Rothenberg coined the term "Janusian thinking"—after Janus, the two-faced Roman god—to describe the phenomenon in which creative insight is sparked by the ability to conceive something *and its opposite* at the same time. In a literal sense, creativity researcher Michael Michalko explains, that kind of thinking inspired Picasso's cubist art, which looked at the same object from multiple points of view simultaneously. Metaphorically, we might think of one of Einstein's breakthroughs in physics, which centered on the question of how an object could simultaneously appear to be in motion and at rest.[1] (If I jump from a roof and release a ball from my hand at the same time, the ball—despite hurtling downward—will appear stationary to me.) The discipline of imagining something and its opposite forces us to probe deeper: What if something we assume is true actually isn't? Why do we do it this way? Is another way possible? Why not?

It's hard to tap into Janusian thinking when you're an insider in the field, however. Bringing a fresh perspective from a different profession or tradition can often lead to major creative breakthroughs. The best practices of one discipline might expose the shortcomings in another. Borrowing a technique and applying it to a new question, or cultivating a renaissance mentality, might provide surprising insight. Ultimately, you can't afford to see problems the same way everyone else does: difference becomes your competitive advantage.

LEARNING FROM OTHER FIELDS

Sometimes your past training in other fields allows you to ask questions, or make connections, that others resist. Eric Schadt started his career as a mathematician—which, as it turns out, was perfect training for his eventual role disrupting the field of biology.

Several years ago, Schadt gave a lecture at Columbia University. Five minutes into his talk, he recalls, a professor stood up and declared, "'I think nobody should continue listening to what this guy has to say.' He said he was going to leave, and everybody else should, too." What could prompt such vitriol toward someone who's published more than two hundred peer-reviewed articles in top scientific journals and been named one of "the world's most influential scientific minds" in a prestigious study?[2]

For the Columbia professor and others, Schadt has become a lightning rod because of his view that classical biology—"the idea that we can understand a living system by understanding each of its individual pieces"—is looking at the world the wrong way. When Schadt decided to enter a Ph.D. program in biomathematics, he had to take remedial classes to catch up; given his focus on advanced math, he hadn't studied biology since high school. "What became immediately clear to me," he says, "was how simplified the writers of biology textbooks were making biology out to be." Biology, he thought, was far more complex than even its own practitioners were acknowledging. And with that knowledge came his opportunity to differentiate himself, build his reputation, and make a contribution to science.

Around 1998, the study of biology changed dramatically with the development of technology allowing scientists to rapidly sequence RNA and DNA and to isolate and measure the activity of certain genes. As Schadt explains it, "Biology went overnight from taking a whole lab to characterize the activity levels of a single gene—you could spend years on that one gene for one disease—to doing that one gene plus thirty thousand other genes in a single day, and for low cost. It was clear that this capability was going to completely transform biology from a qualitative to a quantitative discipline." Most of his colleagues weren't prepared for this new reality; biologists hadn't been trained to think quantitatively and were ill equipped to deal with vast amounts of data.

But Schadt, who had a master's degree in pure mathematics and had studied computer science as an undergraduate, was ready. Working at a pharmaceutical company and nearing the completion of his doctorate, he began proposing ways to leverage the new technologies, but he was "completely shut down. Nobody wanted to fund [his ideas]; they used to criticize them as 'fishing expeditions' and said, 'You're just casting a line. You have no hypothesis, and you just see what you find and make up a story around it.' It was mostly very derogatory."

But he was convinced of the importance of what he terms "the new biology," which takes a holistic look at systems and employs Big Data and other technological advances to gain perspective. Studying genes, Schadt explains, is like studying social networks: you can certainly learn about a person by studying them individually, but you can learn a lot more if you understand who they're talking to and what they're doing with them. Biologists got lucky years ago when they discovered certain genes that definitively caused certain conditions, like the protein mutation that marks cystic fibrosis. But most conditions are far more complex, and you need massive amounts of data to find the subtle correlations.

He began running some small experiments to showcase the possibilities, and his results won converts—slowly. In Schadt's case, it took fifteen years for the ideas he and a small group of allies were advancing to become mainstream. But they've certainly arrived, earning Schadt a prestigious position running Mount Sinai's Icahn Institute for Genomics and Multiscale Biology (where I've consulted for him), recognition as one of the world's most cited scientific researchers, and laudatory write-ups in *Esquire*, *The New York Times*, and elsewhere.

As Schadt's experience shows, initially it's harder to advance in a profession when you're coming from outside. The resistance can be fierce, and sometimes it's years before your ideas gain currency. Others will perceive your lack of experience in the discipline as a liability. *What does he know about biology, anyway?* There will always be people who have more experience—the people who majored in biology in college, and went straight through on the prescribed course. Your outsider status and new perspective, however, can turn your ignorance to your advantage.

Schadt recognized that with the new technologies available, biology could advance quickly—if biologists were willing to think more like mathematicians and computer scientists. Most of them weren't. He understands the resistance. "In some ways, you're questioning their very existence," he says. "It's the fear of the unknown, the fear of not being able to successfully compete." Most successful professionals are invested in the status quo that brought them to prominence. But when times change, new opportunities arise. If you're willing to seek out new ideas and stare down the haters (like the Columbia professor so agitated by Schadt's presentation), you can see connections and insights that are invisible to others.

Part of becoming a thought leader is recognizing that all your previous experiences—your professional training, your innate skills, your upbringing, your hobbies—factor into how you see the world. Like Schadt, you can make your status as a newcomer an advantage, rather than a weakness. If you can study deeply enough to gain mastery, but still retain an outsider's perspective and willingness to question assumptions, you can become great by writing your own rules.

ASK YOURSELF:

- How can you leverage your past training to bring a new perspective to your current endeavor?
- Could the perspective of another field shed light on the questions you're working on now? What would mathematicians (or chemists or philosophers or political scientists) say about the problems or opportunities you're facing?

- Thinking beyond what you're doing now, what other areas have you always been curious about? Are there a lot of people with your background in those fields, or could you contribute a unique perspective?
- Have technological advances made something possible in your field that wasn't before?
- How can you gain the skills you need to take full advantage of that?
- What questions are you able to ask (and perhaps answer) now that you couldn't before?
- What change or trend is most upsetting to the elite in your field? Why are they so upset—and can you get in on it?

ADAPTING TO A NEW SITUATION

When facing a challenge, ask yourself: How can you fill the gap between what's available now and what people actually need? Is there anyone, anywhere, who has solved a similar problem? When you look to what others have done, you can often find unlikely sources of inspiration. You don't have to reinvent the wheel; you can simply adapt the most relevant parts to new circumstances.

Just as Eric Schadt saw the limits of classical biology and was determined to find a better solution, another Eric—entrepreneur Eric Ries—began to ponder how he could improve start-up culture. He'd worked on plenty, and witnessed massive amounts of time and money spent creating products that, in the end, no one wanted to use. It was a heartbreaking waste. In his quest, Ries hit upon another facet of combining ideas—the ability to take specific best practices from one field and give them just enough of a tweak so that they fit into a very different context.

The failure of many start-ups to thrive was, in some ways, an efficiency problem. The traditional gold standard for that was lean manufacturing, a methodology embraced by industrial giants like Toyota that streamlined and improved business processes. But that wasn't quite right for Silicon Valley, Ries decided. "When there's not a long and stable operating history from which to make accurate forecasts, beating the plan isn't cause for celebration," he told me in an interview for the *Huffington Post*.[3] "In fact, successfully executing it often leads to failure because you're fulfilling a bad plan." It would have been a terrible mistake to borrow lean principles and assume you were improving productivity because you were making *more* things—when, in fact, they might be the *wrong* things.

But Ries realized he could salvage the concept for start-ups, and tap its full potential, by shifting the question. Instead of using lean to improve production, you could use it to improve your decision making: "The goal is efficiently figuring out what stuff to make [in the first place]," he says. He began reading up on lean principles, and—drawing on the work of thinkers like Berkeley and Stanford lecturer Steve Blank—applied them to the start-up experience. Ries started blogging, anonymously at first, to test his ideas. Drawing on the failures he'd seen up close, he urged readers to adopt concepts like creating a "Minimum Viable Product" (an initial, stripped-down version) to test demand, and then "pivoting" (i.e., changing course) when necessary. Ries recognized that the old ways of doing business didn't work for the new tech context, so he created new ones. His book-length mashup of lean methodology and entrepreneurial culture—*The Lean Startup*—became a massive best seller, and in the process sparked a movement of techies looking for a better way. As of this writing, there are nearly 1,400 Lean Startup Meetup groups in 472 cities and 70 countries around the world, drawing together 357,000 people. Just as Ries made lean principles relevant and useful in a new context, you can look for problems in your own field that don't have very good solutions. What's missing? Are there other disciplines where you can look for inspiration? Even if the lessons aren't exactly transferable, is there a core idea that you could modify just slightly? How could you tweak it to become relevant in your industry?

If your advice works, as it has for hundreds of thousands of Lean Startup adherents, you'll have a base of fans eager to spread the gospel.

ASK YOURSELF:

- How have other industries solved this problem? How can you learn more about the techniques they use (informational interviews, reading business books, etc.)?
- Can those strategies be imported into your company or field? What would that look like? What would be easy or hard to fit into the existing culture?
- How could you tweak the ideas so they're even more effective?

SEEING DIFFERENTLY

Think about every experience you've had in your life: your friendships, hobbies, romantic relationships, travel, summer camps, internships, jobs, books you've read, and concerts you've attended. How can you fully tap the wisdom you've gained? Most of us think far too narrowly when it comes to our professional lives. At work, we'll bring in skills we learned during college, or experiences we gained through past jobs. But in this 24/7, mobile era, there's no longer an airtight distinction between the personal and the professional. Too often, we don't bring our full selves to work—and that's a mistake. The things that make you a fantastic employee or entrepreneur are frequently what you learned in off-hours, whether it's the time management skills of being a parent, the adaptability and curiosity that comes from backpacking around the world, or the focus that comes from gaining mastery at a hobby, whether it's tennis or chess or poetry or computer programming.

If you want to create genuine insights, you can't keep doing the same thing, thinking like everyone else and offering up recycled tidbits. In the last section, we talked about the value of combining ideas. Sometimes it's important to go even further. You need to be able to *see differently*, and that means not just mixing disciplines, but becoming a person whose perspective is so broad, it defies categorization.

Paco Underhill started seeing differently one day when he was waiting in line at the bank. He flashed back to the previous week, when he'd been standing on a roof, terrified.

"There was a stiff wind blowing, and I was installing a camera and I could feel the building rocking in the breeze," he says. An urban planner working for the nonprofit Project for Public Spaces, he helped cities rewrite their zoning ordinances to make them more livable. But in order to know what policies would generate the desired results, he had to gather data. And that meant going onto roofs and installing time-lapse cameras that would track the pedestrians and cars below. There was only one problem: he was afraid of heights. Up on that Seattle rooftop, "I got really scared. Why had I chosen a profession that involved facing my fears so often?"

A week later, he was back in New York and waiting in line. A long, long line. "I was getting angrier by the moment because I could see something wasn't working, and I realized the same principles I'd been using to look at how a city worked were ones I could take inside a bank or a store or some large public building." He realized his firm could consult for businesses—and if his plan worked, he wouldn't have to scale roofs ever again. But his boss wasn't interested. So in 1977, Underhill launched his own consultancy, Envirosell, with the groundbreaking proposition of applying the principles of urban planning and anthropology to retail environments.

He pulled from another aspect of his diverse background to win early clients. He was part owner of a New York City nightclub, and one night met the head of Epic Records. Underhill made the pitch: "I said, 'I think I can deconstruct a music store,' and he said, 'Send me a proposal.'" Months passed, but eventually he got the call. Just as pedestrians moved in predictable ways across public parks, customers would move through a record store in a consistent pattern. If you understood how to break up bottlenecks, encourage people to linger in a certain area, or motivate them to notice a particular detail, you could dramatically increase your returns.

"Do you want to sell singles? Put them at the right height for a ten-year-old to look at," says Underhill, recalling his early recommendations. "In an era where you sold both LPs and cassettes, people would shop the LPs first and then look for the cassettes, so it created an uneven traffic pattern in the store. If you even out the traffic, you'll better your conversion ratio. It's logical step after logical step." Today, Envirosell continues to advise retail clients, but has also moved into the online realm, tracking consumer behavior on their clients' Web sites. Even on the Internet, the same questions apply: What makes a customer linger? What makes them turn away? Where do they get stuck? Finding the answers to those questions is a mix of both art and science, something Underhill mastered because of his cross-disciplinary training.

He even draws from his college experience to create new insights for clients. He was one of the first male students admitted to Vassar, traditionally a women's college, which made him particularly attuned to the differences in how men and women perceive things. "If you understand women, whether you're selling lingerie or technology, that's critical to your success," he says.

Seeing differently is a quality he values in his employees as well. Today, the top executives at his 140-person company have a theater background. In his experience, they fare much better than MBA students, who arrive with "preconceived notions." In other words, the best employees for Underhill's corporate firm usually don't come from a corporate background. He's looking for innovative ideas, which often spring from living at the intersection of multiple worlds—like urban planning, nightclubs, theater, and business. When you integrate multiple skills, experiences, and identities, you no longer fit into neat categories. You're not moonlighting in another discipline; you're seeing the world differently because it's not through one lens (an actor, a physicist, a doctor). Instead, you've adopted so many perspectives, each is shaped by the others, and no one else can replicate that exact mix. A unique point of view means you're likely to find ideas or opportunities that other, more conventional thinkers may overlook or ignore.

Underhill didn't start his career with a conscious plan to apply urban planning and anthropology to retail stores. But he kept his mind open to opportunity, and unusual connections. Waiting in line at the bank, letting his mind wander, he suddenly saw the possibilities. It wasn't just fusing two fields, or two ideas, together. It was everything. Underhill's business life was a reflection of who he was and how he saw the world.

If you want to develop breakthrough ideas, something outside the norm, you need to be willing to live outside the norm. At times, that can subject you to scorn; many biologists still aren't happy with Eric Schadt. Even when you're not being attacked, you may be greeted with a subtler form of skepticism; Underhill founded his own firm because his previous boss didn't see the potential in his idea. What skills and attitudes do you want to cultivate in your own life? Who do you want to become? (To Underhill, it made perfect sense for an entrepreneurial anthropologist to own a rock club.) The more you become yourself, rather than following someone else's plan, the greater your chance of doing something different that makes a lasting impact.

ASK YOURSELF:

■ Are there parts of your background or résumé that you consider "irrelevant" or out of place? How can you integrate them back into your professional life in a new way?

■ How can you see the challenges in your field through someone else's eyes? What would a woman say? Or a child? Or a rock musician? Or an environmentalist? Considering their perspectives may allow you to see the issue very differently.

■ For the next month, how can you use the new ideas you come across as a lens through which to view or evaluate your industry?

5

Create a Framework

When you're grieving, all you can feel is the sharp pang of loss. It's almost impossible to see the bigger picture, or even to believe that the pain will end. All we have is our intense, personal experience. Elisabeth Kübler-Ross's research on the stages of grief provided a way for us to handle and share these overwhelming experiences of loss. Understanding the structure of that experience—knowing that denial, anger, bargaining, depression, and finally acceptance are part of the package—helps those of us in the middle of grief feel a sense of control and gives others a shared language to discuss loss.

Similarly, Abraham Maslow codified the "hierarchy of needs," articulating the factors that motivate humans. His theory makes intuitive sense; before he formulated it, almost anyone could have told you that finding food and water is necessary, but certainly not sufficient, for a happy life. But Maslow gave a clear structure to those ideas, creating his iconic pyramid showing that while physiological needs are primary and essential, once they're fulfilled, people can concentrate on subsequent levels of necessities: from safety to love to esteem to self-actualization.

When you create a framework that helps explain an amorphous and mysterious experience, whether it's grief or human motivation, you've made an important contribution. People can now understand their lives, and the lives of those around them, with a broader lens. Sometimes you do it by elucidating the principles behind a phenomenon. What are the phases or the steps involved? What is the process by which something occurs, or the formula by which you can create something? Sometimes it's creating a structure that melds the philosophical and the tactical, telling people what to do and why. And other times, what the world needs is an operating manual: something short, fact based, and explanatory that helps people accomplish a certain task. If you can explain things well and make them relevant to a broader audience, you can become a recognized expert.

ELUCIDATE THE PRINCIPLES

If you want to make a mark in your field, try to spell out the fundamental principles behind it. Surprisingly often, the central tenets of a field have never been consciously articulated. For example, people had been enjoying myths for millennia, but Joseph Campbell took the initiative to break down the patterns of the "Hero's Journey" and show why certain stories that applied those principles (like *Star Wars*) were so resonant in our cultural imagination. If you're the one to articulate the hidden structures or rules in your field, you'll help others, and you'll also guarantee that almost anytime the elements of your profession are talked about, you and your theories will be as well. You can do this by breaking down a phenomenon's common features (the most successful entrepreneurs have X, Y, and Z in common), structures (the best screenplays follow this particular narrative arc), stages (like Kübler-Ross's progression of grief), or principles (as Gary Chapman articulates in his well-known relationship book *The 5 Love Languages*).

When Robert Cialdini began studying persuasion, he realized the fundamental principles behind it hadn't been articulated. "I was an easy mark for the salesperson that would come to my door, or fund-raisers asking me to donate to causes I'd never heard of," he recalls. He'd never intend to buy their magazine or donate to their charity. But he always did. "I wondered, *how did it happen?*" He knew it wasn't the merits of the product that prompted him to buy, so it had to be their technique. What were they doing?

To find the answer, he went undercover as an aspiring salesperson and got trained on how to sell insurance, portrait photography, vacuum cleaners, and cars; he even interviewed cult recruiters. Through his research, he developed another breakthrough: the discovery that all of the various persuasion techniques boiled down to just six universal principles. He became the first person to systematize the factors behind influence, laying out how **reciprocation, commitment and consistency, social proof, liking, authority**, and **scarcity** can motivate others.

Why did Hare Krishnas famously give passersby a flower before asking for a donation? Cialdini argued that the reciprocation impulse makes it almost impossible to say no, even when you don't want the flower in the first place. Why am I more likely to do you a favor if I've already done you one in the past? The commitment and consistency principle makes me feel invested in you on an ongoing basis. Why are we more likely to sign on for a charity event if we see that prominent people are on the host committee? That's because of social proof—our natural human inclination to follow others' cues on how to behave. And we've probably all given money to a cause we don't care about because a friend we like asked us, we've followed "doctor's orders" on the basis of their authority, and we've gone into a moderate frenzy to acquire something in scarce supply.

No one had really been looking for a "solution" to the problem Cialdini solved. Most people assumed persuasion was simply the product of stirring rhetoric, or inborn charisma, or—more ominously—pressing on someone's unique weak spots. But Cialdini realized he could create a framework to help people explain a phenomenon that had heretofore been mysterious. That meant that anytime someone mentioned influence from that point forward, he was mentioned right along with it.

Codifying a system, he says, "is important because it provides a set of touchstones that we can return to for every new situation we face. *What's the system here I need to apply?*

What are the principles of influence that might be available to be more persuasive in this new situation?" If you can show others a new, clearer way to view the world, you can make a significant impact.

ASK YOURSELF:

- Has the overall nature of your field been articulated? If not, could you do it?
- Is there an aspect of your field that hasn't been adequately defined or codified? Go back to the basics:
  - ▸ What problems seem mysterious?
  - ▸ How are we defining the problem, anyway? Are there limitations to that definition?
  - ▸ What secret would you most like to figure out?
  - ▸ What phenomenon do you wish you understood?
- Have you noticed a cluster of related phenomena? Can you group them together or give them a name?

CREATE AN OVERARCHING FRAMEWORK

Another important element of codifying a system is showing how it works in practice. To inspire others to take action, it's useful to blend the philosophical (how does it work in theory?) with the tactical (how can I actually get it done?). David Allen has succeeded in building a massive following for his Getting Things Done (GTD) methodology because he consciously tries to blend the conceptual and the granular. "The main difference in what GTD does is that it underlines the principles beneath the best practices; it doesn't just give tips," he says. "I think some of the other people who have become knockoffs of GTD took the principles of 'write it down and make lists' and don't really focus on the core elements of what it is." If you can create a holistic framework that engages people's beliefs and shows them how to take action, you can create a valuable tool in their lives.

Even before the start of the social media era, questions of how to stay organized and productive were pressing concerns. So when Allen's productivity guide *Getting Things Done* was released in 2001, he found a receptive audience. In his early days in business, he linked up with a small business consultant named Dean Acheson—not the former secretary of state—who became a mentor. Acheson would try to conduct off-site retreats with clients about the future of their business, but often found "their psyche was still hung up on three weeks ago, [and] the piles on their desk that weren't being handled or managed very well," recalls Allen. His solution, which Allen later adopted, was encouraging them to write everything in their head down on paper, and then creating a "next action decision" to map out how they'd move forward.

With Acheson's permission, he began to develop and expand on this framework of capturing and processing tasks. Allen had become fascinated by the idea of models, and how they could be used to improve performance. "What could you do without having to change yourself a lot?" he wondered. "How do you point your smarts to get better results? That tied into my interest in how to find a model that pretty much works for everybody and that everybody could use, no matter what business they were in or at what level."

GTD tried to address the fundamental problems facing busy executives. "You don't need time to have a good idea, you need space," says Allen, "and you can't think appropriately if you don't have space in your head. It takes zero time to have an innovative idea or to make a decision, but if you don't have psychic space, those things are not necessarily impossible, but they're suboptimal."

For years, Allen developed his theories by working as an executive coach. "It truly took thousands of hours," he says. "I was well beyond ten thousand hours . . . and once you've spent twenty thousand or thirty thousand hours, deskside or walking people through exercises in seminars around the world, you go, 'I think I've kind of figured this thing out,' and have watched it produce results." That time in the trenches resulted in his now-famous framework.

Allen believes there are five stages "to get anything under control, whether it's your kitchen or your country." First, you need to **collect** everything you're dealing with— gather all the scraps of paper, and jot down all the random ideas or notes. Next, you **process** it. If it can be done in less than two minutes, do it. (*Send a congratulatory e-mail to Tim! Download that album you've been meaning to buy!*) Otherwise, plan if you'll delegate it to others or defer it. Then, **organize** what you've gathered, because many projects, such as writing a book, are more complicated than just one step and require lists and folders to keep things straight. At this point, you **review** everything weekly to ensure you're staying on top of your projects and obligations, and finally **do**—that is, make choices about your next actions.

You want people to take action, but they'll only be inspired to do so if the plan you set out for them seems doable. If you focus on articulating both the big picture (what they should do) and the tactics (how they can do it), you'll help others break through their fear or inertia and get moving on the changes they need to make to succeed.

ASK YOURSELF:

- How can you help others in your field do things better or more efficiently?
- What are the principles behind the best practices you espouse? Can you explain the underlying premise of your philosophy?
- What are the simple things that are stumbling blocks for too many of your colleagues? What's holding back their progress?
- Can you break your recipe for success into discrete steps?

WRITING THE OPERATING MANUAL

Robert Cialdini and David Allen both codified valuable new principles in their fields. But in order to make a contribution, you don't necessarily have to come up with a breakthrough idea on your own; you may be able to popularize something great that's been underappreciated. If you find an "idea worth spreading" (to borrow the TED conference's popular phrase), ask yourself if it has spread as far as it could, or if its reach is being limited by some external factor. A brilliant concept could be hobbled by the wrong messenger or arcane language, and with creativity, you may be able to hasten its success—and become recognized for your own authority on the subject. You don't have to be the world's expert in order to become *an* expert. You just have to be willing to help move the idea forward in your own way.

That was the case for John Allen (no relation to David), who'd been a bicycling enthusiast since he was a teenager in the 1960s. His world was rocked when he read John Forester's 1976 book *Effective Cycling.* "Having read Forester's book, my riding style changed in a matter of a week," says Allen. "I'd rate him as a genius in terms of his understanding of the subject." Forester pioneered the concept of "vehicular cycling," in which bicycles, rather than being cordoned off from cars, operate as vehicles on the road and abide by the same rules. Counterintuitively to some, vehicular cycling often improves bicyclist safety because the drivers of cars are typically watching for other cars, so if you're on your bike in the middle of the road, even if it feels exposed, you're more likely to be noticed by (and safe from) the other drivers.

On the other hand, bicycling on the edge of the road, inches from the parked cars, leaves you exposed to "dooring" by careless motorists exiting their vehicles or "right hooks" from turning drivers. Not to mention that many infractions bicyclists usually get away with—like riding the wrong way on a one-way street—are simply dangerous. If it's not right for a car, Forester argued, a bicycle shouldn't be doing it, either.

There was only one problem with Forester as a vehicular cycling evangelist, however. Known for his irascible personality and inability to tolerate fools, he quickly became controversial. Some rejected his message largely because of the messenger. He had developed a Big Idea, but it struggled to gain traction, thanks to his forceful and heated internecine policy debates with other bicycle advocates.

Firmly believing in Forester's ideas and hoping he could help them catch on, Allen started writing for *Bicycling* magazine by the late 1970s, mostly science- and fact-based pieces about the mechanics of safe riding, and penned a 1980 book, *The Complete Book of Bicycle Commuting*. Allen's work builds on Forester's theories of vehicular cycling, but advances them in important ways. He stripped out much of the combativeness that limited Forester's reach, appealing to cyclists who may have been alienated by Forester's tone. And almost accidentally, he gave the market something it turned out was very much needed. In 1987, his publisher asked if he'd consider writing a condensed version of *The Complete Book of Bicycle Commuting*—a forty-six-page booklet articulating the principles of vehicular cycling, and more.

Allen agreed, and his short manual eventually came to the attention of transportation officials from the state of Pennsylvania, who decided to republish it as the *Pennsylvania Bicycle Drivers' Manual*. Eventually, Florida, Arizona,

Idaho, and Ohio signed on and also adopted Allen's manual as their own; today, it's sold nearly 400,000 copies.

It may seem incredible that something as simple as riding a bike could warrant a stream of official statewide manuals and eye-popping sales. But, as Allen points out, "Bicycling is a field where most people have no instruction and don't do it well." As elementary schoolers, we're taught by our parents to stay upright on a bike and imagine that's sufficient, but riding in traffic—as opposed to circling your backyard or driveway as a kid—is an entirely different phenomenon. Chilling news reports of cyclist deaths often stir fears that urban cycling is inherently dangerous, but a better understanding of "bicycle driving" can prevent errors and save lives.

A bicycle operating manual might seem unnecessary to some, but it's proven enormously successful. Even when something seems as "simple as riding a bike," it's likely there's more under the surface. Allen helped others recognize that in an accessible and useful way—and stay safe on the road in the process.

Popularizing ideas is an important role. Malcolm Gladwell has become a best-selling author of works like *The Tipping Point* and *Blink* by bringing the research of academics like David Galenson (an economist who studies creativity and the arts), Mark Granovetter (a sociologist who looks at social ties), and John Gottman (a psychologist studying marriage) to the masses. Just as Forester may have been a bit too feisty for popular consumption (his personal Web site begins with a paragraph about "discriminatory laws" and a "bogus safety argument")[1], most academics don't have the fluid writing chops of Gladwell, a *New Yorker* mainstay and a captivating storyteller. He brings their research to life and ensures that it will be recognized by a far broader audience than they could command on their own. When it comes to breakthrough ideas, says Des Dearlove of Thinkers50, "Originality can be overrated. We see a lot of thought leaders who are synthesizers now," citing examples like Gladwell and Daniel Goleman, who popularized the concept of "emotional intelligence." "These guys bring communication skills and an ability to bring complex ideas and make something out of them, but it's not their [original] research." If you see a need in the marketplace—an idea that deserves to be heard—and you can help translate it, that's a clear route to thought leadership.

Of course, you don't need to be a prodigious literary talent or a *New Yorker* staff writer to popularize ideas. If you can be the person who introduces lean methodology to your company, or who reads industry journals and suggests new innovations your business can incorporate, or who loves TED talks enough to organize a local TEDx conference, you can follow the same formula.

ASK YOURSELF:

- Have you read all the seminal books in your field? If not, make a list and start reading them. What did they leave out? What additional knowledge could you contribute?

- Is there a way to distill your field's fundamental knowledge? What are the most essential pieces you'd put into a short guide?

- What do most people misunderstand about your field? What errors do they make, and can you help redirect them?
- Can you create an "operating manual" for your area of interest? What does everyone need to know or do? What are the steps they should follow?

SYSTEMATIZE SPREADING THE WORD

Creating a framework means helping others think about a topic—whether it's influence, productivity, or bicycling—in a new way. It can also involve creating a system that enables your idea to spread. How do you make it easy, even desirable, for others to get involved? That's the process the Reverend John Gibb Millspaugh began one day when he was stuck in traffic. That afternoon, amid the exhaust fumes, something clicked. He was a committed environmentalist; he drove a subcompact car, and kept a vegan diet, but with all those cars—not just in front of him, but worldwide—he realized it wasn't enough. His own actions, however well intentioned, weren't going to make the kind of difference that was necessary in the world. How could he engage others?

Food, he thought, could be an important place to start. "Food justice issues are something everyone can make an immediate difference in, in terms of understanding how their lives connect to this larger issue," he says. "Talking about nuclear proliferation, people might care about that, but not be sure what they can do. But we're eating every single day. It's not like a hybrid car purchase that only some of us can afford, and it might come around every few years. With foods, it's multiple times a day. It's an empowering way for people to get involved."

As a Unitarian Universalist minister, he also recognized the spiritual implications. "It's easy to have a romantic, sentimental attachment to communing with nature," he says, "but it's much harder to consider how our daily choices are impacting the climate and environmental degradation and animals. I did try to frame this as a spiritual practice." It would be powerful to get the denomination behind his efforts. But he couldn't simply lobby for a top-down proclamation. Millspaugh knew the congregants would rebel. "UUs are pretty antiauthoritarian and they like to think for themselves," he says. "They don't like to be told what to do."

He had to put a structure in place so the issues could be discussed, and people could come to their own conclusions. Along with some like-minded colleagues, he created a compendium of congregational resources, such as lists of books and movies, worship guides (including relevant hymns and sample sermon excerpts), articles, and information about how to design a potluck where people could discuss "ethical eating." They then started the ball rolling on a four-year "study process," a staple of UU parish life. "We tried to equip people and enable them to talk about these issues in an informed way in a group setting," says Millspaugh.

He knew he couldn't force his ideas or his will onto the conversations—it had to come from the bottom up, but he provided the tools. "I involved people by not providing any answers at the beginning, and valuing them as thinkers," he says. "Everyone's got to make their own decisions, and we're not going to end up at the end of this process with a doctrine or a definition of what ethical eating looks like, but all of us are invited to figure this out for ourselves." As a result of the conversation, some members might decide to become vegetarian or vegan. Others might vow to eat more organic food, or make an effort to visit farmers' markets and seek out local produce. Others might cut back on their red meat consumption, or do nothing at all.

For Millspaugh, it's the process that mattered. "It's not about arriving at a certain place. It's about keeping an open question as to how you're impacting the earth and looking for ways accessible to you, given where you are in your life, to make a positive difference." There's not one "right way," he says. "You can't understand the impact of your food choices on all who are affected, the food system is so complex." But if you can shift your perspective to think about the experience of animals, or farmers, or factory line workers, you may decide to make different choices.

Three years into the study group process, in June 2011, the Unitarian Universalist denomination passed a statement in support of ethical eating. "I don't think the statement itself will influence people much," says Millspaugh. "But it exists in UU history and activists can use it as a foothold for the causes they're working on. When someone says, 'Our congregation should be thinking about stopping purchasing Styrofoam' and that's dismissed as over the top, that activist can say, 'Our entire denomination passed this statement, and this is part of what it means to be UU.'"

Today, more than 40 percent of UU congregations have participated in Millspaugh's ethical eating study groups. Political action will probably be necessary to change America's food culture, he believes, but consciousness-raising comes first: "Until we have a larger mass movement around food justice issues, the politicians aren't going to be incentivized to make change." He leveraged the power of his denomination, and the organizational structure of its study group process, to create a conversation he knew needed to happen. "It can be difficult to know if change will come in ten years or in ten generations," he says. He's motivated by his faith to keep going. "My fuel for activism became much more abundant when I realized it's not about the quantity of change I can achieve in my lifetime; it's about doing what there is to do, with the faith that I'm doing my part."

Change begins with the individual, and Millspaugh was certainly doing his part to save the environment, but the challenge was enormous, and he needed to bring other people on board. From discussion manuals to worship guides, he and his colleagues created a structure that made it easy for others to ask similar questions and have difficult conversations. Is there an issue you truly care about? Something too audacious for you to accomplish on your own? As it was for Millspaugh, it can be powerful to think through the resources you have to get others involved, whether it's a shared denominational affiliation, access to a media outlet (even nontraditional ones like blogs or podcasts), or connections you may have developed over time. How can you make it easier for others to dive in? We can't fight the biggest problems alone, but they're often the ones most worth tackling.

- How can you make it easy for others to learn about and share the message? Are there tools you can create (such as Millspaugh's worship guides and recommended reading lists)?

- How can you leverage the power of your institutional affiliations to get momentum for your issue?

- Are there communication mechanisms (such as newsletters or conferences) or public platforms (resolutions, endorsements) you can use?

BUILDING A FOLLOWING AROUND YOUR IDEAS

CREATING SOMETHING OF real value to others is the starting point of thought leadership—but you can't stop there. You could have the best idea in the world, but it won't have much impact if no one's ever heard of it. There's just too much noise and competition out there for good ideas to gain traction by themselves. If you genuinely believe in it, it's incumbent upon you to build a strategy for spreading the word.

In part 2, we'll talk about how to build your network—the critical **one-to-one** connections that form the foundation for your movement. Then, we'll turn to building an audience, which allows you to grow your influence by communicating **one-to-many**. We'll talk about key strategies—from blogging and social media to writing a book—that can help you attract like-minded followers. Finally, we'll discuss the apex of movement building: creating a community around your idea (which allows it to spread **many-to-many**). When enough people start to care about your idea, they connect around it, become evangelists, and exponentially increase the likelihood that it will take root more broadly in the culture.

The idea of building a following around your idea may seem intimidating. Remember, you're not entering this process alone. You don't start by tossing your idea out blindly and seeing what happens. Instead, you first share it with a trusted inner circle that supports you and can help you refine it. Only then do you expand outward and begin testing the waters, seeing who else is interested. Your job is to nurture your idea—accepting refinements that make it stronger, but retaining its essence and integrity as you share it with ever-expanding circles. Eventually, it will be strong enough to thrive on its own, and it will become part of the broader conversation. At that point, you'll have succeeded.

6

Build
Your Network

You can't create a movement on your own. If your idea is going to spread, you need to build a following around it. The good news is that you probably already know people who believe in you and your vision. Most likely you have friends and family who could be enormously useful in getting the word out, connecting you with the right people, or leveraging their social networks on behalf of your idea. These existing networks are an important starting point because it's the people who know us who are usually the most willing to help.

You can make a list of the obvious candidates—people you see often, or with whom you have a particularly close connection. It's worthwhile to start talking with them about your idea to get feedback and get them on board. Then, take the time to look through your address book or database to remind yourself about more distant colleagues who may also be able to lend a useful perspective or connect you with resources. A quick e-mail or a coffee date can be an invaluable starting point as you begin to think about how to spread your idea.

Whether your existing network is large or small, it is important that you nurture it and take action to expand it. In this chapter, we'll talk about a variety of ways to cultivate the connections in your life, from creating a professional development group to networking through interviews to leveraging your alumni affiliations and connecting through charitable causes. Find the strategy that feels right to you and take action, because—though networking sometimes gets a bad rap for being a sleazy, one-sided attempt to extract value—when done right, it benefits everyone. Of course you'd like help spreading your idea, and if they believe it's a good one, they'll want to assist. But when you also focus on how you can help them achieve their goals, you become not just a "networker," but a trusted friend and valuable colleague.

CREATING YOUR PROFESSIONAL DEVELOPMENT GROUP

Becoming a recognized expert in your field is a challenge, but it's much easier with the support of a strong peer network. A group of trusted colleagues can help you refine your ideas, provide honest feedback, and share insights and leads. They'll also provide you with a dose of inspiration—you can see their successes and learn from them—and support when you face discouragement or setbacks. Most of us have some helpful professional contacts, but they're not necessarily an active community focused on helping one another. Very few people luck into their own personal Bloomsbury or Harlem Renaissance; instead, you'll likely need to take action to create such a network. That's what Kare Anderson did on two separate occasions.

She started her career as a journalist, working for *The Wall Street Journal* and NBC News. Seeking to enhance her skills, in 1988 she formed a professional development group made up of six other reporters. They'd trade advice on how to cover breaking news, and who the best sources were. "I had more, better quotes that contributed to a better story, and that was huge," she recalls. "And it felt really wonderful to do that back for them, that feeling of reciprocity." She's no longer a journalist—given the decline of the industry, half the group has actually left the profession—but they've continued to meet every single month for more than twenty-five years, offering advice and referrals. "When you're meeting monthly and you continue to do so, you know so much, you talk in shorthand," she says. "Together, we can bounce ideas more clearly off each other because we know each other so well and give candid feedback."

Today, Anderson makes her living as a professional speaker, so in 1994 she started a monthly speakers' group as well. To be as efficient as possible, each meeting has a specific structure. The participants convene on Skype and speak in the same order each month; each member offers up a need (something others can help them with) and a resource (help they can offer to others). Their colleagues then respond if there's a match (you need a Web site designer and I know a great one). That's a typical meeting. When crisis hits, personal or professional, the group comes together. When one member was up for a big job, the group focused like a laser, just as they did when another member's daughter died.

The group has certain rules that members adhere to. It's confidential; there are no referral fees; and when you make a commitment, you're expected to keep it. Members keep notes on their colleagues' needs and resources, and will often bring them up months later if a new opportunity has arisen. "You ask yourself, 'Am I giving as much as the others are?'" she says. "It sets a standard." It's not a quid pro quo, but there's an expectation that members will contribute.

Anderson has found a variety of professional benefits. She's gotten new speaking gigs on the strength of referrals from group members, and they trade technology tips about products and services that might prove useful in their business. Mostly, she says, the benefit has been developing such deep and intimate professional relationships over the past quarter century. "You look back on notes you've taken, and it's a way of realizing how much we've evolved," she says. "There's a record of witnessing each other's lives in mutually beneficial ways. It's made me a better person because of the mutuality at the center of it."

Do you have enough people in your professional life who really know you? The bias in most discussions about networking is toward meeting more people, going to more cocktail parties, and trading more business cards. But sometimes depth can be as important, if not more so, as breadth. In a fast-moving world, it's a powerful touchstone to have people in your life who have known you for years and watched you grow and progress. Sometimes we learn the most about ourselves through the eyes of others we respect and trust. Could you develop a deep professional community like Anderson's? It may be essential to the success of your idea.

ASK YOURSELF:

- Who do you respect among your peers? Make a list of them—people you know who work in your industry or sphere. For each, write down one action you can take in the next one to three months to deepen your relationship (schedule a call, take them out for lunch, connect at an industry meeting, etc.).

- Could you benefit from developing an active peer group? Who would you want to invite into your group? Which colleagues would fit together best? Are there shared interests or values? Don't immediately announce your idea and issue invitations; create informal opportunities for them to mingle to see if there's chemistry and a positive exchange of ideas.

- What rules or shared understandings would be most important, from your perspective?

- What kind of insight or help are you hoping to receive—and what kind could you give to others?

GROWING YOUR NETWORK THROUGH INTERVIEWS

Kare Anderson brought together a core group of colleagues to support one another professionally. That's an important first step in sharing your idea with the world. But in order to gain traction for our ideas, most of us need to think strategically about how we can also connect with influential people we *don't* already know. After all, unless you're Sheryl Sandberg looking to launch *Lean In* (with massive wealth and robust connections in Silicon Valley and Washington, D.C.), you probably need further help in getting the word out. You may need to connect with top business leaders, or journalists, or venture capitalists, or the advocacy community. Any prominent person is going to be busy and overwhelmed with requests, however. You need to be crystal clear in identifying whom you'd like to meet, understanding your value proposition (i.e., why they should make time to meet you) and communicating that effectively, and then building genuine connections with them. That's what Bay Area attorney John Corcoran did through his blog and podcast, *Smart Business Revolution*, in which he interviews thought leaders he admires.

It's a major investment of time, but Corcoran sees several professional advantages in creating his podcast series. First, it's providing helpful information to listeners he'd like to connect with, such as entrepreneurs who might be potential clients. When he meets one who mentions an issue they're facing, he can usually talk about it intelligently, thanks to his interviews. "I'm not an expert in Facebook marketing or e-mail marketing or how to use LinkedIn for business, but because I've done those fifty interviews, it provides me with an opportunity to help people even before they're a client of mine," he says. And while he's never gotten a client out of the blue because of his blog and podcast, he's certain it's led to repeat business because he's staying top of mind.

Corcoran also benefits from the knowledge he gleans from interviews. "It's professional development as marketing," he says. "I'm learning and educating myself as a business owner, and yet for the hour I spend learning, I can then take that recording, package it up, and send it out to the world as a podcast that will exist for infinity for other people to benefit as well."

Most important, "The value to doing podcasts is relationships," says Corcoran. The interview gives him an excuse to connect with interesting guests and hopefully develop a longer-term connection with them. As one of his guests, I had a firsthand look at how effective this was at building relationships. I met John when he introduced himself to me at a conference. He had clearly done his homework—he knew I was a speaker and what I looked like, and was able to build rapport immediately by citing a political campaign we'd both worked for. He invited me to be on his podcast, and we struck up a friendship that's led to our collaborating on several *Forbes* blog posts and my inviting him to be a guest speaker at a workshop I conducted. I'm also not the only new contact he built a relationship with.

The previous year, he had an audacious goal: connecting

with best-selling author Daniel Pink. "I started doing things to get on his radar screen, so I could build a relationship with him," Corcoran recalls. He signed up for Pink's newsletter, read his blog and all his books, and connected over Twitter. "Eventually I got up the nerve to ask him to be on my podcast. He was guest number five, and I'd hardly had any big names prior to that."

He asked at the right time—by design, because he knew authors are more likely to grant interview requests when they're promoting their books. Pink, who had just launched *To Sell Is Human*, agreed to the chat. "If you do it over Skype, you can see each other, and it's almost like you're in a coffee shop, except you're three thousand miles away," Corcoran says. "It's helpful [to the conversation] if there are visual cues. But I also want to build a relationship with them; I want them to see my face, even though Dan was in Washington, D.C., and I was in San Francisco."

Pink himself is an occasional podcaster, and extols the practice as a hybrid of recreation, networking, and professional development. "I don't play golf, so it's basically my golf—almost a leisure pursuit of mine," he told me. "It was something I was always meaning to do, a poor man's radio show with people I'm interested in talking to. It's totally fun. I can talk to them for forty minutes and share it with other people." Pink has used his own podcast to connect and strengthen relationships with other successful authors such as David Allen, Tom Peters, and more.

Corcoran promoted his interview with Pink heavily on social media, and made sure to get a ticket to his upcoming San Francisco book tour event. The event turned out to be massive, with nearly five hundred people in attendance. But to Corcoran's delight, when he got to the front of the book-signing line, Pink greeted him first: "Hi, John." Says Corcoran, "It was just so cool that here is this author that I admired, whose book I was a big fan of, and because of the podcast and social media, I was able to build and nurture a relationship with him before I'd ever met him face-to-face." Corcoran's strategy is great for connecting with well-known people, who are far more likely to agree to be interviewed (which means their ideas can spread), rather than accepting an invitation to have a stranger "pick their brain" for free for an hour. But where he truly excels is in the follow-up. Many people would conduct the interview and leave it at that; after six months or a year, the celebrity guest may dimly remember their name, but that's about it. But, as Corcoran points out, the secret is turning that initial connection into a real relationship, as he did with another podcast guest, Internet entrepreneur Andrew Warner.

Corcoran researched him intensively prior to the interview, studying up on his background and reading everything Warner had written. When Corcoran learned Warner was soon moving to San Francisco, he jumped into overdrive: This was an area where he could add value. He provided Warner with restaurant recommendations, advice about neighborhoods and apartments, tips on upcoming events, and introductions to people in the city.

Corcoran even helped Warner's wife, a consultant for socially conscious companies, make professional connections in the Bay Area. Eventually, the Warners invited Corcoran and his wife over for a double-date brunch, solidifying the relationship. "My relationship with Andrew started with the podcast interview," says Corcoran. "I never would have had any excuse for having an hour of his time." But today, they're friends.

Corcoran follows up, whereas most people don't. But most important, he doesn't take a one-size-fits-all approach to his networking. If he wants to build a relationship with someone, he makes an effort to understand them first. He asks, "What does this person need right now?" In the case of Pink, it was publicity for his new book, so a podcast interview was a welcome invitation, rather than an onerous obligation. And Warner, moving to a new city Corcoran knew well, needed help with the basics—where to eat, where to live, and how to get connected to the entrepreneurial community. High-level people are bombarded with messages and requests all day, so it may—even if you're trying to do them a favor—come across as another burden if you don't think it through carefully (do they *really* want to meet that person you're suggesting?). But well-timed, thoughtful help is invaluable, and earns you a place at the table.

Canadian social media consultant Debbie Horovitch took a similar approach to making connections through her own interview series, conducted via Google+ Hangouts on Air. Like Corcoran, she offered business authors the opportunity for broader exposure. But she also realized the technology itself—which allows for live, multiperson webinars that can be recorded and uploaded to YouTube—was an inducement. She was an early adopter, and many of the guests she invited had never done a Hangout before and wanted to learn how it works. The connections she's made have already been transformative for her business; one author has offered to connect her with his publishing house, and she's been featured in a book by one of her Hangout guests, Mike Michalowicz.

If you want to make the most of your half hour (or however long you're speaking with your guest), follow Corcoran's and Horovitch's lead: choose the timing of your invitation wisely. Many top leaders and authors are so busy, they turn down almost all interview requests until the exact moment when they have something they need to promote. (Tim Ferriss, author of *The 4-Hour Workweek*, reports that he gets a thousand e-mails a day, which he describes as "unreal" and "brutal."[1] It's no different for most other well-known people.) Your request is far more likely to be accepted if it coincides with the release of a new book, TV show, product launch, or the like. Create a target list of people you'd like to connect with and start reading their blogs and following them on social media so you can learn about the projects they're working on and determine when they'd be most receptive.

Next, prior to your interview, do as much research as possible. When Corcoran wanted to connect with Daniel Pink, he subscribed to his newsletter, read his blog, connected on Twitter, and read all of his books. That's an investment of dozens of hours—but it paid off when Pink greeted him by name at the event, and, when I asked Pink about Corcoran months later, he remembered exactly who he was. Indeed, through his blog and podcast, Corcoran has steadily been building his own reputation as a thought leader. Now he's often the guest on other popular podcasts—and he still does his homework. When I heard him interviewed recently on John Lee Dumas's *EntrepreneurOnFire* show, during a segment in which Dumas asks all guests about their favorite productivity hack, Corcoran mentioned an Internet password tool and told Dumas, "I cannot believe this was not taken before . . . it wasn't on your list . . . six hundred plus interviews and no one's mentioned it!" Think about that for a moment, because it's significant. Corcoran took the time to listen to enough of Dumas's podcasts to know he was going to be asked the question about his favorite tool. And beyond that, he took the time to review the list of more than six hundred recommendations on Dumas's Web site and identify one that no one had yet mentioned. Dumas was clearly delighted, mentioning that he used the tool every day as well. That's the level of preparation that sets you apart, and ensures you'll be noticed and remembered.

Finally, Corcoran's point about the importance of keeping in touch is crucial. If you follow up, stay on their radar, and find ways to add value, you can turn an initial meeting into a lasting connection. Though we had mutual friends, the first time I spoke with Mike Michalowicz—who ended up featuring Debbie Horovitch in his book—was when I interviewed him for my *Forbes* blog.[2] We kept in touch by e-mail, and several months later he had a speaking engagement in my city and invited me to breakfast. Several months after that, he invited me to join a professional speakers' networking group he was starting, and we've subsequently vacationed together with the group. I met Harvard Business School professor Amy Edmondson briefly—for perhaps a minute—at a conference, and asked if I could interview her for my *Forbes* blog as well. That gave me the opportunity to meet her at her office, and she was impressed when I turned our one-hour chat into three separate blog posts.[3] That kick-started a friendship, and we've now been to dinner at each other's houses, and she blurbed my first book. In the past two and a half years, as of this writing, I've created more than 250 blog posts for *Forbes* alone. The vast majority of those posts are interviews with authors and business leaders, and (as Corcoran and Horovitch also experienced) it's given me the excuse to meet the people I'd like to connect with. Writing for a brand-name publication helps, but it's not essential. Even if you're writing for your own personal blog, the vast majority of people will agree to an interview; one podcaster friend told me that no interviewee had *ever* asked him how many listeners he had. Because your interview will go online and will be findable by search engines, it's less and less relevant whether you're backed by a major media brand. If you are, that's nice; if you're not, don't let that stop you from trying this powerful form of relationship (and brand) building.

To successfully spread our ideas, most of us will need to cultivate new relationships in addition to our core group of trusted colleagues. Connecting with busy people is never easy, but if you make it a consistent part of your schedule and show others why it's worth their while, you can build a substantial network faster than you might imagine.

ASK YOURSELF:

■ Who are the well-known people you'd most like to connect with? Make a list. How can you begin researching them in depth (read their books, subscribe to their e-mail newsletter, etc.)?

- What strategies can you use to make a connection (interview them for a podcast series, join an organization where they're involved, attend a conference where they're speaking, etc.)?
- Once you've made a connection, how do you plan to stay in touch and keep the relationship alive?
- How can you add value to these high-level contacts? What do they actually need (publicity for their upcoming book, connections to other thought leaders or reporters, restaurant recommendations, introductions to potential clients, advice about an upcoming trip they're taking, etc.)?
- Is there a new channel or platform that you can use to connect with people (as Horovitch used Google+ Hangouts)? They may be particularly inspired to sign on because they'd like to learn about it, too.

LEVERAGING YOUR AFFILIATIONS

Corcoran and Horovitch grew their networks through podcasting and Google+ Hangouts, but there are also "old-fashioned," analog strategies that are surprisingly powerful. One of the best is leveraging your affiliations to connect with like-minded people, because your shared history or point of view allows you to build trust (and a solid relationship) quickly. One of the most popular *Forbes* posts I ever wrote was an interview with Robert Cialdini—yes, that's how we first connected—called "How to Get Someone to

Like You Immediately."[4] The secret? He says it's to find a commonality—any commonality—fast. It could be something as simple as the fact that you live in the same neighborhood, or you both like running. One particularly powerful bond is having a shared alumni connection, something consultant Robbie Kellman Baxter learned firsthand. She estimates that half her consulting business comes from fellow Stanford Graduate School of Business alums. That isn't just good luck; she's made Stanford the core of her volunteer efforts in the nearly twenty years since graduation. Baxter's involvement with Stanford has two advantages. The first is branding. As one of the top business schools in the country, it's incredibly selective—and the fact that she was accepted and graduated sends a strong message about her competence. As researchers Matthew Bidwell, Shinjae Won, Roxana Barbulescu, and Ethan Mollick revealed in their paper—fantastically named "I Used to Work at Goldman Sachs!: How Organizational Status Creates Rents in the Market for Human Capital"—it's true that "working for a high status employer provides workers with a valuable signal of ability which helps them to secure better jobs in the future."[5] The same is almost certainly true of one's association with a top-tier university.

Unless someone is reading your bio or your résumé, they wouldn't necessarily know where you went to business school (or that you have an MBA at all). It would also seem awkward or overly self-promotional to mention one's Stanford connection out of the blue. But Baxter's alumni volunteer work gives her a great opportunity to talk with others, including potential clients, about the events she's speaking at or organizing, leaving them with the impression: *this is an accomplished professional.*

Second, Baxter's alumni work directly builds her network, giving her an easy opportunity to make connections with interesting new people. "It's such a natural community, and we have this shared history," she says. "The reason it's good for your business is that you're able to form genuine relationships with like-minded people very quickly, and to me, that's the definition of good networking. There's a kind of trust: I know what you went through because I went through it, too."

Her Stanford volunteer work started in the smallest of ways, running the class notes column for the alumni magazine. Over time, she stepped up her involvement, helping to organize reunions and speaking to other alums who were also interested in becoming solo consultants. Soon, Baxter realized that while other alumni clubs (like Harvard's) were active in the area, there wasn't robust programming for Stanford alums in Silicon Valley, because of the assumption that alumni could access events on campus. She figured there ought to be some events tailored specifically to their needs.

That's why she launched the Strategy Breakfast Series, "a quarterly breakfast that we would open up to all alums. We'd hold it on or near campus, and talk about some issue related to business strategy. For the first couple of years, I organized all of them." She picked hot topics—like the future of mobile payments—that would be sure to attract the local start-up crowd. Her hard work also benefited her visibility. "I was meeting people, up in front of the podium, and my name was often being sent out to the entire alumni community, so it was great for building awareness and credibility."

As a result of her service, she's become a go-to speaker and volunteer—resulting in her being asked to join a prestigious advisory committee for the school, the Women's Initiative Network. "It was a really great opportunity, and I don't think I would have been invited if I hadn't done so much work with Stanford already," she says. Through her work on that committee, including helping to organize an annual conference, she's built relationships with influential alumni.

The key ingredient in her volunteering and networking success, says Baxter, is her passion for the school. "There is the prestige of continuing to be associated with such a great institution as Stanford," she says. "But for affiliation to be effective, you have to have a genuine desire to help that organization. It has to come from an authentic place. I've thought many times, 'Would I still be doing the same things for Stanford even if I were suddenly phenomenally wealthy and no longer needed to have any clients?' and I would."

Baxter's example is important for several reasons. First, she chose to get involved with a cause she really cared about. If you hated your college experience or are joining a group only because your boss is a member, your lack of interest will eventually show through. It takes energy to participate, and sometimes you're called upon to do unpleasant things (get up at six A.M. for a charity run, or stay to clean up after an evening meeting). If you care about the cause, that sense of mission can get you through; if you're neutral or tepid, it's hard to justify the investment. You'll be asking: *is this how I really want to spend my free time?*

Next, it's important for the tasks themselves to feel enjoyable to you. The alumni association could probably use plenty of volunteers to chair fund-raising dinners or monitor the finances of local chapters, but that wouldn't have been as rewarding to Baxter. Because she's volunteering, she can choose the scope of her engagement and concentrate on the tasks that are enjoyable, like connecting with friends from her class (through reunions and the class notes column), networking with fellow alums (through the speaker series and one-on-one coffees), and sharing her professional expertise (through lectures and webinars).

Finally, she chose to "go deep" with one cause. If she'd dispersed her volunteer efforts, she probably would have met more people at first—going to different events and mingling with different crowds. By investing in Stanford, she came to be recognized as a leader and was tapped for high-visibility roles that ensured she wasn't just meeting people one-on-one; people she'd never talked to now know exactly who she is.

Building on alumni connections is a great strategy, but not everyone went to a prestigious university, of course. Like Baxter, however, everyone can think about ways to get deeply involved with some kind of cause or organization, many of which don't require specific credentials to join, but which create a strong sense of affiliation. Over the years, I've participated in a number of networking communities. When I lived outside Boston, I was a member of my local chamber of commerce and often attended their networking events; I also actively participated in an online message board for solo consultants and organized periodic meetups of group members from New England.

Similarly, you could join (or create) corporate alumni groups from current or past companies you've worked for, conferences or events that you attend, or demographic affiliations you share (black professionals, female attorneys, etc.). Finally, an often-overlooked networking opportunity is the civic and charitable groups you support, the topic we'll turn to in the next section. The goal of all of these strategies is to give the other person a reason to see you as a colleague, not a stranger. You're known by the company you keep, so make sure it represents you well—and that, since you're involved, you're maximizing the value of that affiliation to meet people with shared values.

ASK YOURSELF:

- What are the strongest brand affiliations you possess? Have you worked for a prominent company, written for a major publication, attended a prestigious school, won a major award, built relationships with prominent leaders, etc.?

- When was the last time you updated your LinkedIn profile? Update it with your relevant affiliations to make it easier for people to find you, and to showcase your background.

- If you don't currently have strong brand affiliations, what's your target list? It may be too late to attend an Ivy League college, but with effort, you can certainly get a blog or op-ed published in a major newspaper, or take a leadership role in a prominent civic association.

- What other organizations do you care about or would you like to get more involved with (such as business networking groups, the local chamber of commerce, etc.)?

- What are the ways you can "go deep" with your key affiliations? Is there a way to volunteer your time or get more involved?

- Are there ways you can maximize the networking potential of your affiliation? Can you volunteer for the membership committee (where you have to reach out and connect with participants), rather than a more behind-the-scenes role?

THE CAUSES YOU SUPPORT

If there's a cause you care about, there may be ways you can integrate it into your professional life, benefiting your community and growing your network at the same time. Serving on charitable boards is a great opportunity for networking and skills development, but it's even more powerful to ask: *how can I integrate a commitment to service into everything I do?* If you can figure out how to live out your values in every aspect of your business, the relationships you build as a result will be among the strongest and best you have, because they're founded on a shared commitment to something larger than yourself.

I got to know the real estate agent Thalia Tringo when we served together on the board of East Somerville Main Streets, a civic improvement group outside Boston. But that wasn't the only cause she supported. She's an active board member of the Somerville Homeless Coalition, and donates

$250 to charity for every real estate transaction she completes. "I'm not a religious person," she says, "but I try to tithe a percentage of my income. That's hard to do when you're a Realtor [because of the variable income stream], so when I started, I decided I'd give a certain amount for every transaction, and that way I'll know I'll have done my giving."

Like John Gibb Millspaugh, however, the real endgame for Tringo is inspiring others to take action. She recruited a client to the board of the Homeless Coalition, and inspired another to get involved with Community Cooks, a charity that mobilizes local volunteers to cook healthy meals to supplement the food that's available at homeless shelters. "One client does it with her two daughters, and they know they're doing it for another mother and her children," she says. She's mobilized residents on her street to help a neighbor threatened with homelessness while battling cancer, and actively promotes a sense of community by seeking out owner-occupant buyers who want to be engaged in local civic life.

Her reputation for civic-mindedness has become a core part of her brand, and her client base—including me—draws on many people she's met through her volunteering. "Today, I had a closing with somebody I would never have met, except we serve on the board of the Homeless Coalition together," she told me. Tringo's charitable involvement "was never really a marketing strategy," she says. "It's a good marketing strategy, but that wasn't the intent." When you take action on the causes you care about and connect with people around them, you can create a powerful network and a professional reputation that precedes you.

- What charitable causes are you most passionate about? Where could you get involved? What skills could you bring to the table in helping them? Set aside an hour in the next week to do online research and determine which nonprofits may be a good fit.

- Are any of your contacts involved in charities you're interested in? If so, can you make a plan in the next month for an informational interview to talk about their efforts?

- As with Thalia Tringo's $250 donation for every completed real estate transaction, is there a way you can integrate charitable involvement or giving into everything you do professionally?

- How can you encourage your clients, colleagues, or even competitors to get involved in charitable pursuits as well?

- How can you get involved in a charity you care about over the course of the next three months?

Build
Your Audience

7

So you've built your network, creating a brain trust of people who are eager to help you refine and share your ideas. Now it's time to scale up. To make a true impact, you have to build a larger following—and thanks to the Internet, that's never been easier. As John Hagel of Deloitte's Center for the Edge told me, creating content and interacting online is essentially a way to put out a beacon so that like-minded people can find you. "You can use the power of social media, in particular, to amplify the signal of what you're working on," he said. "What's your passion, what excites you, what questions are you grappling with? You can put a light out to others: here's somebody we ought to reach out to."[1] Creating content and interacting—whether it's on a blog or via social media—is a way to let others know you're out there and have ideas to share. Instead of one-to-one, you're now going one-to-many.

THE POWER OF BLOGGING

If you're just starting out on social media, start by *listening*. Follow the people you admire on Facebook, Twitter, blogs, or other platforms, and see what they're talking about and how they present their ideas. As you become familiar with the issues of the day and begin to formulate an opinion about them, you can begin to share your own ideas. Are there viewpoints that are being overlooked? Step up and present them. Do you disagree with the way an issue is being presented? Here's your chance to right that wrong.

If you want to be known for your ideas, you need to share them: period. In the past, you had to wait to be "chosen" by a newspaper or magazine editor; now you can start writing and see what happens. At worst, it will be slow going and you'll feel like no one is discovering your blog—though that's not the end of the world, because what matters is having the *right* people read it, and you can always proactively e-mail out links (*"Jake, I wanted to follow up on our conversation about online marketing. I thought you might be interested in this post I wrote last month called 'Five Ways to Improve Your Internet Marketing.' Hope you find it helpful!"*). At best, you can quickly establish yourself as an expert because others can see for themselves that you're knowledgeable. Blogging—or video blogging, if you prefer—is one of the most powerful ways to draw people to you and build a following around your ideas.

That was a lesson I learned when I attempted to get my first book published. Prior to the fateful *Harvard Business Review* blog post in 2010 that led to *Reinventing You*, I had written three different book proposals. I secured an agent, which already-published friends told me was the hard part, and waited for a deal to pop. Despite nibbles of interest, including a lengthy back-and-forth with one publisher, they all eventually said no: I simply wasn't famous enough.

Of course, they didn't say it quite like that. But in the wake of the 2008 economic crash and a resulting purge in the publishing industry, editors had gotten *very* conservative when it came to first-time authors. I had always imagined that I could write a high-quality book that would, in turn, bring me recognition. What my repeated rejections taught me was that you first have to create your own recognition—the publishing world's preferred term is "platform"—that virtually assures you can sell ten thousand or more copies of your book, mitigating almost all their risk. If you can find a way to come to publishers with an audience already in hand, they'd love to work with you. Which is why my lowest point, perhaps, was when one editor told my agent, "I really like this manuscript, but Ivanka Trump has a book coming out on a similar theme, so we want to see how that one does first."

With no hope of traveling back in time to find a more famous father (mine was a psychiatrist in small-town North Carolina), I realized I needed to step back. The book would have to wait. Instead, I embarked on a "platform building" campaign. The core of my own strategy was blogging—a direct way to share ideas and build a community around them.

I started with my "warm leads"—friends who already blogged for prominent publications. I had to persevere for months, asking different people if they'd be willing to introduce me, and patiently but persistently following up. Eventually, my friend Michael Silberman successfully connected me with his editor at the *Huffington Post*. That was a good start, but HuffPo is better known for its political coverage than its business writing, so I wanted to try to find another outlet to complete my "portfolio." I had numerous friends let me use their names with their editors at various business magazines, or who even introduced me directly—to no avail. Occasionally, I'd get a halfhearted response from the publication's Web editor, asking for a list of pitches, which I'd spend hours crafting overnight . . . only to receive no response for months, if ever. I persisted, sure that eventually I'd find someone who was open-minded enough to realize that having a former journalist write for them—for free—wouldn't be so bad.

Fast-forward more than a year. I wanted to buy a new bike, but decided I should sell my old one first. I advertised it on Craigslist and sold it to a woman who—quite rightly—had Googled me to make sure I was legitimate. "I see you're a business consultant," she told me, as I was handing over the goods. "You know, I work at *Harvard Business Review*." Bingo! As we completed the transaction, I casually asked, "How does someone get started blogging there?"

I had to follow up several times, but she eventually introduced me to one of the editors. Thanks to the stream of pitches I'd been developing (which had been ignored by the other publications), I had plenty of ideas and a few sample posts. The second one they ran became *Reinventing You*, and changed my life.

The ability to share ideas with a new audience is one of the most compelling aspects of blogging. "The blog is something I *get* to write—I don't *have* to write," says well-known author Seth Godin, who posts on topics ranging from marketing and branding to living a meaningful life. "I get to write every day, and it reaches over a million people. It's a really powerful tool for me that I would write, even if it was read by five people. The act of writing clarifies my thinking a great deal."

He believes far more people should take up the practice. "The fact that I don't have a lot of competition in what I do is astonishing to me," he told me. "We say to every salesperson, every marketing person, every engineer, every CEO: 'Here you go, here's this free platform. If you say something that's worth writing, people will read it. Do you want to use it?' And they say no. What's that about? I literally don't understand why people are eager to put 140-character things out on Twitter, but aren't willing to actually share thoughtful, generous, useful insight in a more permanent platform."

As Godin indicates, blogging isn't the easiest platform around. It takes five seconds—maybe thirty if you're particularly fastidious—to create a tweet. It can take hours to put together a smart, well-crafted blog post, marshaling your points into a cogent 500 to 800-word article. (Godin's daily posts are often unusually short, sometimes only 200 words, but are known for their pithy insights.) Much has been made about the decline of blogging among teens and young adults.[2] Well, *of course*. That doesn't mean blogging as a platform is dying or irrelevant. It means that it's hard, and if teenagers have access to an easier way of communicating, usually involving snapping photos or taking videos, they'll do it. That's not a mystery; it's a competitive advantage. If you're willing to expend the effort to create well-crafted content, you'll distinguish yourself in a crowded marketplace where many people are serving up easy morsels, and you're taking the time to create something of substance. Far more people share content, rather than produce it. If your posts stand out, it's your material that will be passed along.

Another drawback of blogging—for the lazy and impatient—is that its results aren't instantaneous. Despite my early success with the HBR post, it's taken years and hundreds of articles written to result in a steady stream of corporate speaking invitations, for instance. Godin agrees that it takes time to build a blog audience and for it to "pay off" in a traditional sense. "If you say, 'I'm not going to do anything if it doesn't pay off in four days,' now I know why you're not using a blog, and you've just told me a whole bunch about yourself, right?" he says. "You told me you want to be picked, meaning having Oprah call or HBO call or someone call, and you want it to pay off right away or you're not going to do it."

But taking the time to share yourself in a substantive fashion is an investment in your long-term reputation. "When I run into the Mitch Joels or the Tina Eisenbergs of the world," Godin told me, citing the prolific marketing and design bloggers, "I know who they are before I meet them. Because they've been whispering in my ears for months or years, and they're so generous about the way they approach the world. Why *wouldn't* you trust those people more [than those who haven't been blogging]?" One of the mantras of business networking is that you should always try to give value before you receive it. But many people overlook the fact that giving doesn't have to take place in person; many people feel grateful to Mitch Joel (or whoever their favorite blogger is) because of his steady stream of insights, and are far more likely to want to help him, whether it's by buying his book, reviewing his podcast on iTunes, recommending him for a speaking engagement, or hiring his digital marketing agency.

Above and beyond the reciprocity impulse (which Robert Cialdini identified as being one of the cornerstones of influence and persuasion), that positive feeling toward our favorite bloggers is compounded by a phenomenon known to social psychologists as the "familiarity principle" or the "mere exposure effect." As an array of researchers have shown, most famously Robert Zajonc of the University of Michigan and Stanford, repeat exposure often leads people to feel more positively about a given person or object.[3] If I like a stranger simply because she rides the same commuter train in the morning and I see her every day, I'm certainly going to feel even more positive about someone who shares useful insights with me day after day.

Starting to blog is easier than ever. In 2014, LinkedIn began rolling out a feature that allows all members, not just their select group of celebrity influencers, to create blogs on the site. The functionality is simple—if you understand Microsoft Word, you can easily create a post—and your posts automatically appear on your profile. That's the perfect credibility statement for potential clients or employers who are checking you out and want to verify how knowledgeable you are about your industry. Another way to get started is by contributing guest posts to other blogs. Make a list of the blogs you read and search on the site to see if they accept guest contributions (if you aren't sure, you can e-mail the Web editor and ask). Create a post that fits their guidelines—no one will run a five-hundred-word post if their format is set up to feature three-thousand-word pieces, or vice versa—and then send it in.

If after testing the waters with a few guest posts you decide that blogging is for you, it's time to get serious. Depending on your goals, you may want to set up your own blog. Increasingly, WordPress is the platform of choice—and it's free, except for a small annual fee that allows you to route your blog back to your own Web site (for instance, mine is http://dorieclark.com/blog/), which is advisable because it makes it easier for people to find and remember. If you want to build up traffic on your own site—perhaps you'd eventually like to make money on advertising revenue, or draw people in to sell products—you can use your blog as the go-to spot for your readers.

Alternately, you could expand your reach initially by blogging for outlets that already have a reader base, which is my strategy in writing regularly for places like *Forbes, Harvard Business Review,* and *Entrepreneur.* (I still post my articles on my own blog, but use it more as a repository and archive.) Either strategy is good; it primarily depends on your goals and how/if you plan to monetize your blog, which we'll discuss further in part 3. If you plan to make money directly off your blog, you'll want to maximize readership there, but if you're intending to make money through indirect means, such as speaking or consulting, as I do, it may be better to increase your overall visibility on other sites. Whatever your blogging strategy, the most important thing is to get started. Your ideas can't gain traction if no one knows about them; blogging is a way to reach others and get them on board. For Godin, who has built a massive following and is now able to command large speaking fees, his continuing devotion to the unpaid work of blogging is a way to give back. "It's a privilege," he says. "My goal with the blog is to put ideas into the world that change conversations among people that I care about."

ASK YOURSELF:

- What do you want to write about? If you don't already blog, make a list of possible topics. Try to come up with ideas for ten to twenty posts at the outset, to get you started. Think about the most common questions people have about your field, misconceptions people hold, emerging trends you see, or interesting shortcuts or ways to "hack the system." What tips have enabled you to be successful? What current news stories have implications for your industry?

- In the next week, set aside ninety minutes on your calendar and write a post. You can share it on your own blog (if you have one) or via LinkedIn. See what response you get. What ideas do readers seem to connect with?

- What blogs do your target audience read? Make a list of outlets you'd like to write for, and research online to find the e-mail address for their Web editor.
- Ask your friends or search LinkedIn: Do you know anyone who writes for those publications? If so, see if you can score an introduction. If not, write to the Web editor cold, send him/her a few links to existing posts you've done (so they can make sure you write well), and offer a few catchy suggestions about what you'd like to write for them. Reach out to at least two in the next month.

GO WHERE THE PEOPLE ARE

Blogging is a critically important tool for getting the word out about your ideas. But it's not the only one. Robert Scoble initially gained fame as a blogger, but in recent years—similar to my strategy of seeking out blogs with a preexisting audience—he's shifted his focus to social media. "Part of it is looking at where the audience is," he says. "You've got to figure out where they *are*. It's not about how to get them where you want them to go." Indeed, social media can be a powerful force in connecting with people and, if you're already blogging, leveraging the impact of those posts by ensuring that they get seen more widely.

When Scoble realized the immense and growing popularity of platforms like Facebook and Google+, he decided to go all in, and shifted his efforts to interacting there. "People thought I was an idiot," he told me during an early 2013 interview for my *Forbes* blog, "but I saw social networks were going to be more important, and it turned out to be true. A year ago [in 2012], I had 15,000 followers on Facebook and now it's 43,000, and on Google+ it went from zero to 2.9 million. I saw it was worthy to focus all my energy in these new areas."[4] It's important to realize that you don't have to be on every platform, but it's a good idea to pick at least one or two to focus your energy on.

Scoble also advises joining a platform early: you're commonly cited, and it's easier to build an organic, viral following. "If you come in late," he says, "you have to spend more energy to get a network of one thousand people than I did." And the network he's built is massive—at one point, drawing 730,000 comments on Google+ in a ninety-day period.

Listen carefully to the buzz in your community. What is your target audience reading? Where are they spending their time? Is there a new app or platform everyone's talking about? Just as Debbie Horovitch identified Google+ Hangouts as an opportunity because few, if any, social media strategists specialized in them, you can distinguish yourself by becoming an early adopter. It's not a strategy for everyone; if you're not comfortable with technology, you may not want to waste your time pioneering something you don't actually enjoy. But if you like exploring the "new new thing," it could be a winning move for you.

Note that there are risks associated with jumping on board

early, however. If the platform stagnates or fails, your efforts may be wasted. Notable social media experts Chris Brogan and Guy Kawasaki both wrote books touting Google+ shortly after it was launched. But despite Robert Scoble's success with the platform (which demographically leans male and tech savvy), I imagine they have to be disappointed by its failure to take off among the general public. As I'm writing this, it's generally an afterthought when it comes to most people's social media usage.

Its muted popularity wasn't a big deal for them, however, because they place multiple bets, writing tons of content and frequently pumping out full-length books. It's a strategic gamble: if Google+ were a runaway hit, they'd be recognized experts on a medium everyone wanted to learn about. If its performance turns out to be lackluster over the long term, they're still experts in a small niche that's occasionally relevant. Like venture capitalists, developing expertise in Google+ was a part of their portfolio, not their entire bet. They're constantly developing other ideas, and continuing to look for the "ten-bagger" (to borrow a phrase from famed investor Peter Lynch) that will exponentially return the time they invest to master it.

Regardless of the platform you choose, you have to build an audience by creating interesting content, having conversations and interacting with readers, and staking out a defined niche for yourself. What do you want to be known for? Use social media to start conversations with the content you create, and engage with others who are writing or sharing information about related areas. "Even if you're into the weirdest, most esoteric thing in the world, there are probably at least fifty other people in the world into your thing," says Scoble. "Build a club and find them, and put blog posts on Google so people find out."

A technique that can further accelerate your platform-building efforts is cultivating relationships with the traditional media. Being quoted in the mainstream media is useful because they often still have large audiences, even in an era of fragmented reading and viewing habits. Plus, their third-party validation lends credibility to you. If you're quoted in *The New York Times* or have appeared on the *Today* show, that's a public signal that you're an authority. (When the Associated Press and *Fortune* magazine both called me a "branding expert," that went directly into my bio because while it's vaguely pretentious to call yourself an expert, it's powerful when others do it for you—a principle based on the research of Robert Cialdini and Stanford Graduate School of Business professor Jeffrey Pfeffer that I explore further in *Reinventing You*.)

The era of media consolidation has changed how we should go about building those relationships with journalists, however. A decade ago, my advice would have been to ask reporters out for coffee to get to know them. During a leisurely conversation, you could find out what types of stories they were looking for, offer up your expertise, and perhaps suggest some ideas or pitches. No longer.

Reporters are usually way too busy to have coffee with someone they don't know, and they'll rarely make the effort. It's not laziness; it's simply the reality of their job these days, now that they're expected to file multiple stories a day and can't afford to leave their computer for a moment.

Instead, focus on building your relationship via social media. They'll love you forever if you retweet their posts and draw attention to their work (because more and more, journalists are now evaluated and remunerated on the basis of the page views they generate).

If you follow their stream assiduously, you'll probably find out what events they'll be attending, and you can make a point of popping by and introducing yourself in person. But in order to be helpful and not burdensome, focus on building the relationship electronically at first, and later advance to face-to-face. Once that connection is solidified, they'll be thrilled to know whom to call when they need a comment on a certain type of story, and you'll go from being viewed as a possible nuisance to someone who can be of great help.

Creating content through blogging demonstrates your expertise, and—as we saw with Robert Scoble—leveraging both social and traditional media magnifies its impact. If you're bothering to stay on top of trends and share your ideas through informative posts, you might as well ensure they're being seen by the largest audience possible. Going where the people are helps introduce you to the masses and attract a bigger following.

ASK YOURSELF:
- Where is your audience now? What are they reading/listening to/watching?
- What social channels does it make the most sense for you to prioritize, based on what your audience is consuming and your own personal preferences?

(It's no good forcing yourself to make online videos if you hate being on camera.)

- What new platforms are emerging? Can you jump on board now, before the competition catches on?
- What sort of content should you create in order to "build a club," as Scoble says? What will attract people to you and your ideas?
- Who are the key reporters in your field? Create a media list. Write down all the newspapers, industry journals, bloggers, TV and radio outlets, etc., that have influence in your industry. Now go online and identify the right reporter(s) for each, and create a spreadsheet with their e-mail and phone contacts.
- How can you make those connections? Start following your media list on Twitter. Make a plan to retweet their stories or comment regularly to start building a relationship.

SCALE YOUR IMPACT

When you're thinking about how to spread your idea, scale matters. With only twenty-four hours in a day, and only so much time to respond to messages or create content or take meetings, you have to be ruthless in your prioritization and savvy about how you allocate your time. For many people in traditional jobs, efficiency is nice but outside their job description (you're paid to produce fifty widgets an hour, and that's what you do). But if you have an idea you want to share, you don't have that luxury. You have to ask yourself constantly, "How can I reach more people?" If someone asks Robert Scoble a question via e-mail and he answers them back, that person will be grateful and may think Scoble is smart and helpful, but unless she's a blogger or journalist or extremely networked person, that knowledge won't get around. If you want to build your reputation as an expert publicly, it's far better to follow Scoble's lead and answer questions or share ideas in a way that everyone can see them.

Just as Scoble doubled down on platforms like Facebook and Google+ when he realized they were gaining traction, he also turned to the question-and-answer Web site Quora (in which people post questions, and other users write in and share their expertise). The common denominator? Scale. "I'd rather answer a question on Quora than on e-mail," he says. "A question on Quora can help five people out, whereas a question on e-mail can only help one person out."

I recently received an e-mail from a friend's husband, who was interested in starting a career as a professional speaker. I was glad to offer advice, but realized that he's not the first person to have asked me the same questions. In fact, he might have been the twentieth or fiftieth. So, inspired by Scoble's example, I told my friend's husband I'd respond back in a couple of days—and did so by sending him a link to a blog post[5] I wrote about the topic in response to his questions, which (as of this writing) has been viewed by more than three thousand other people as well.

Scaling the impact also drives other thought leaders, in a variety of ways. It's why Rose Shuman has expanded Question Box throughout India and sub-Saharan Africa, helping thousands more people connect to the Internet. It's why John Corcoran and Debbie Horovitch make their conversations with luminaries available as podcasts and You-Tube videos—building their brands and those of their interviewees.

When Mark Fidelman spends one hundred hours creating a blog post, he wants to make sure it reaches as many people, in as many ways, as humanly possible. That's why he leverages his content by creating infographics, a SlideShare, and even an e-book to support the original material. If you're going to get your idea out there, you can't stop before the finish line and assume that having a brilliant concept is enough. You have to keep pushing and thinking of ways to expand your audience, because that's the only way you can achieve the critical mass necessary for your idea to truly penetrate in a noisy world.

If you can do that, the rewards are enormous. In a globalized society, your ideas can attain greater scale than ever before possible. If you can harness the power of scale and combine it with generosity and a desire to help more people, you'll be unstoppable.

ASK YOURSELF:

- How can you reach more people with your ideas?
- Can you repurpose your content into a variety of new forms, such as infographics, podcasts, Slide-Shares, videos, tweets, Instagram images, etc.?
- Challenge yourself: How can you take one piece of content and distribute it on five or even ten different channels? For instance, you could record a

podcast interview, write a blog post based on your conversation, tweet out the best quotes from the interview, create a SlideShare explaining a key concept that was discussed, and create a one-minute online video explaining your biggest takeaway from the conversation.

WRITE A BOOK

One of the classic ways to get recognized for your ideas is to write a book, ideally with a well-known, traditional publisher. Working with an established publisher, it's easier to get your book covered in the media and stocked in bookstores, you have support in areas you may be less familiar with (distribution, marketing, design, etc.), and there's the credibility of their brand behind you. It's not the only way, however.

Self-publishing, once the forlorn province of those who had been rejected everywhere else, has become increasingly common. Particularly if you're dealing with a niche topic—one the publishers suspect will never reach a *Fifty Shades of Grey*–size audience—it can be an excellent way to get your message out. That's what urban planner Mike Lydon discovered when he self-published his free e-book *Tactical Urbanism: Short-Term Action, Long-Term Change*.

He launched his planning firm, Street Plans Collaborative, in 2009, in the wake of the Great Recession. He quickly learned that cities weren't eager to pony up for large-scale municipal improvement projects. Meanwhile, he'd been observing the growing trend of low-cost experiments (famously, in places like Times Square) where previously traffic-choked areas were reclaimed for pedestrians and bicyclists.

He was fascinated by the emerging DIY ethos, exemplified by citizens taking the streets into their own hands with experiments like planting gardens on vacant lots or painting their own bike lanes onto roads. Lydon began to look into the phenomenon. It didn't even have a name, and most people viewed these projects as interesting one-offs, not a movement. But he sensed a trend emerging amid the new economic reality. Fiscal austerity allowed—or perhaps forced—a greater level of creativity. Instead of ten-year projects, the question became: what can we do in six weeks? Recalls Lydon, "It was, 'Let's get it done, and if they like it, great. If they think it sucks, we'll iterate. It's just paint, and we can put it back the way it was.'"

Reading the blog of a landscape architect named Brian Davis one day, Lydon was struck by his description of one New York City project as "tactical." Says Lydon, "To me, a lightbulb went off. That's exactly what all this other stuff is!" With Davis's permission, he coined the phrase "tactical urbanism." Now he needed to get a handle on what it really meant. He began collecting case studies of local projects from around the world. One goal was to spread the word; another was to "set the record on what's good and what's bad in these projects." As someone who loves cities, he didn't want ill-conceived projects tarnishing the movement's progress. "We wanted to create a definition and help create a clear direction moving forward," he says.

A good example would be the "parklet" movement, an idea that spread over the past decade from Hamilton, Ontario, to San Francisco (where there are now more than forty) and beyond. The idea is to transform parking spaces into an actual park using cheap, accessible materials, such as landscaping and tables and chairs. "They're quick and easy, they make an impact, and in San Francisco, they're adding up to a lot of reclaimed space," says Lydon.

He assembled the case studies into a free e-book available on the Street Plans Collaborative Web site. The response was immediate, with ten thousand views and downloads within the first few months—a massive amount within the small urban planning community. "We realized this collection of ideas was what a whole new generation of people was looking for," he says. "It's not just young people, but people who think differently about what cities can be in this country." It became so popular, he and his partner created *Tactical Urbanism 2*, showcasing even more case studies, and with a partner in South America, they created a third volume featuring Latin American examples. Together, the booklets have been viewed or downloaded more than 160,000 times, establishing Lydon as one of the world's go-to experts on the movement.

When Lydon launched the booklets, his firm was still new and scrambling for business. But the e-books, and the many resulting speaking engagements, have solidified its reputation. "We're becoming known for this work," he says. "It's been a differentiator for us and opened doors." As interest in tactical urbanism grows, Lydon has even started to see communities create RFPs (requests for proposals) that specifically seek firms with that expertise. "We've been hired and sought out for the tactical urbanism component," he says. "And as we build relationships, clients see we have other skill sets."

By naming and—through his exhaustive collection of case studies—helping to define the growing concept of tactical urbanism, Lydon created a powerful brand identity for his nascent firm. That's enabled it to flourish, even in a challenging economic climate, and allowed him to make connections with clients who might have been hesitant to engage a small, untested firm for a major project, but now have built a trusting relationship.

For Lydon, a book was the ultimate calling card, an unparalleled opportunity to showcase his expertise and enable potential clients to test-drive his ideas. Of course, the time investment is substantial. While you could bang out a blog post in an hour or two, a book can take months, and many people lose patience with the process. Some turn to writing groups to help them stay motivated; others are assiduous about blocking out sacrosanct time on their calendar and treating it like a client project. (Personally, I work on my books in four-hour chunks; anything less, and I find it hard to get into the rhythm of writing; anything more, and my attention starts to wander.)

Fortunately, the mechanics of self-publishing are getting easier by the minute; you can use simple self-publishing platforms like Amazon's CreateSpace, which make the process fairly plug-and-play, or create a PDF document and put it up on your Web site, as Lydon did. Guy Kawasaki and Shawn Welch's book *APE: Author, Publisher, Entrepreneur—How to Publish a Book,* a more successful experiment following Kawasaki's book on Google+, provides a useful overview of the process.

It makes sense that an entrepreneur like Lydon would want to showcase his expertise through a book. It may come as more of a surprise, however, that self-publishing can also help regular professionals with their job hunt. After all, hiring someone is a big risk. You have to train them and get them integrated into your company; if it's a bad match, you may have wasted months and tens of thousands of dollars. It's so much simpler if you can hire someone who's a known entity—someone you feel confident will do a great job from the start. You may feel that reassurance if you've worked with a candidate before, or know someone who highly recommends them. But if you don't know them personally, reading their book allows you to vet them and understand where they excel.

Miranda Aisling Hynes always loved to write, so when she was studying for her master's degree in community art and looking for a thesis project, she decided to create a book. She wanted it to inspire regular people, however—not just practicing artists or those inside academia. The term "art" is loaded, she'd come to believe; it signified something rarefied that most people couldn't imagine aspiring to. "But everyone is creative," she says. "Whether they use that creativity is a different issue, but it's an innate human skill like curiosity, and your creativity can manifest itself in any number of ways. . . . Most people do want to be creative; they just had it squashed out of them at some point."

The end result (published under "Miranda Aisling," her middle name) was her self-published book *Don't Make Art, Just Make Something*. She recognizes that self-publishing probably won't make her rich or famous. "I think you have to have realistic expectations about what you're going to get out of it," she says. "It's an entrance [for other people] to my ideas. I haven't really made a profit; I've pretty much broken even." It is, however, helping her achieve her goals. She gave a copy to a friend who worked at a local arts center; he passed along the copy to his boss after he'd finished reading it. When Hynes later applied for a job at the organization, the director was enthusiastic, praising it during her interview and again in front of the entire staff when she went in for the second round. "The book definitely opened the door," she says. She got the job.

She also views it as part of her long-term dream to open a "community art hotel" that connects visitors with local artists. "The more stuff you create—a blog, Web sites, books— the more articulate you become about your passion and purpose," she says. "And the more articulate you become, the more people flock to your message." It's about creating a variety of touch points that can draw people in and keep them engaged. Someone discovering her Web site might order a copy of her book, sign up for her e-newsletter, and perhaps start attending the regular art and music gatherings she hosts. "Instead of building the arts center and hoping the community will come, I'm building the community first and hoping they'll help me make the arts center."

Hynes's strategy is exactly right. As Eric Ries showed in chapter 4, whether your business is high-tech start-ups or community art hotels, it's easy to imagine that if you simply create your perfect vision, others will discover it and flock to it. But too often, that's a disastrous assumption. It's far better to start with an idea, test it, refine it, and build a following around it. That way, when you're ready to go big, you have a core base of support that can help you spread the word and carry your idea far beyond where you could take it on your own.

You start by listening and learning about the issues of the day, as you begin to formulate your own point of view. Then, you begin to share your thoughts via blogging and social media. Finally, as you've built up a following that's interested in your perspective—and asking for more—you can expand those concepts into a book that encapsulates your philosophy and how you see the world. That will be your calling card to attract like-minded people to you and your ideas, and to help ensure that they spread.

ASK YOURSELF:

- If a book could serve as a calling card for you, what message would you want it to convey? What does the world need to hear?

- In addition to spreading your message, how could writing a book help you achieve your professional goals? For Lydon, it attracted clients; for Hynes, it landed her a job. How does a book fit into your objectives?

- How will you make time for writing a book? If you're serious about the idea, set aside time on your calendar and test out different writing strategies (times of day, amounts of time) until you learn what works optimally for you.

- What's your angle? You'll probably need to narrow down your topic by focusing on a particular aspect of your field (as Lydon did with tactical urbanism) or expressing a point of view (as Hynes did with *Don't Make Art, Just Make Something*). Purchase a book like Jeff Herman and Deborah Levine Herman's *Write the Perfect Book Proposal: 10 That Sold and Why*, 2nd edition, to learn what's required to create a solid proposal. Even if you plan to self-publish, rather than submit your proposal to a traditional publisher, the discipline of answering the questions can be useful. Write down two or three angles and test them by talking with friends and colleagues. What do people respond to the most strongly? What seems to be missing from the conversation?

8

Build a Community

Y ou started by building your network—the close colleagues around you who can inspire you and help
you succeed. You moved on to developing an
audience—the true believers who connect with your message and love what you do. Now the final step is turning
those diffuse, individual contacts into a community. The
best ideas don't stay tied to their creators forever; they go
out into the world and make a difference because people
make them their own. Mike Lydon compiled the case studies for his urban planning e-books, but now they're freely
circulating, inspiring activists on multiple continents to experiment with ideas that make communities more livable.
Similarly, your ideas—once they hit critical mass—can become a movement. In this chapter, we'll talk about how to
bring people together, in person and online, who share a

passion for an idea, whether it's empowering creative professionals, building a social justice community, or helping professionals become better at their jobs.

Some who impugn the concept of thought leadership seem to think it's all about self-aggrandizement. That may be true for some, but real thought leaders have an idea they want to share with the world—one they know is important enough to fight for. Of course, it's an accomplishment to have created and spread a powerful idea, and money and accolades may come your way as a result, but the ultimate test of an idea's value is whether others want to take it up and spread it on their own. A great idea is about more than just you. You can begin to create a movement by becoming a connector, or building a platform that allows a community to form. You can become a mentor to like-minded others and bring people together around that point of view, and perhaps strip away the seriousness that so often comes with "community building" and inject a forgotten element of fun that keeps people coming back. Whatever your strategy, the goal is the same: finding new ways to connect people and help them empower one another.

BECOME A CONNECTOR

One of the best gifts you can give is to connect people who can benefit from knowing one another. If you've accrued a wide network, you probably know people who'd like to meet. Taking the time to facilitate it builds your own reputation as a giver, but it also allows amazing new things to happen—conversations, transactions, and innovations that wouldn't have been possible without the introductions you provided. If you can develop ways to connect colleagues or match "buyers" with "sellers" (of any kind), you can create a powerful community that surrounds you, and is grateful to you, but isn't *about* you.

As Peter Shankman built his PR firm over the course of a decade, reporters would constantly ping him. "They'd call and say, 'Hey, I'm doing a story—who do you know?'" Maybe they were looking for moms concerned about their kids' diet. Or a recent grad who couldn't find a job. Or an expert on monetary policy. Whatever it was, and however arcane the request, Shankman tried to assist. It felt good to help out, plus it built up his favor bank with reporters, whom he needed to cover his own PR clients.

But at a certain point, the requests became overwhelming. In 2007, he created a Facebook group to broadcast the requests to interested people, and soon shifted to an e-mail list, which he christened Help a Reporter Out (HARO). By 2010, it had grown to "three hundred thousand people reading my e-mails three times a day," he recalls. "We had a seventy-nine percent open rate, which is ridiculous."

Indeed, most e-mail newsletters hover around a 30 percent open rate, if they're lucky. But HARO, available to subscribers for free, provided an invaluable service: access to reporters who were working on stories and hungry for sources. Journalists would e-mail their request to Shankman ("I'm looking for career experts for a story in *XYZ* magazine, with a deadline of Monday at five P.M."). He'd categorize it ("business") and compile it in a list with other requests.

After it went out, recipients—including other PR firms, small business owners and entrepreneurs, and in-house communications staff at organizations seeking coverage— would scour it for relevant opportunities. They'd click on a link for the stories they thought they (or their clients) would fit, write a short response explaining why the reporter might be interested in talking to them, and submit. The reporter could then review all the responses, and choose whom to contact. Shankman had become the perfect middleman, linking two parties who were extremely eager to connect.

Of course, the service was an invaluable help to his rivals, other PR firms. When Shankman started, he was doing it for free, but it quickly gained in popularity, and companies proactively reached out to him to see if he'd accept advertising. Within two months, he'd sold out his ad space six months into the future.

He realized he had a phenomenon on his hands. The advertising revenue allowed him to hire two staffers to help manage the growing volume; they worked out of his apartment. Meanwhile, his own brand was skyrocketing. "My name was in your in-box three times a day, so you knew who I was," he says. "It was immediate brand recognition. Reporters got tremendous value out of it. And if I had a client [to pitch], reporters would listen to me because they trusted me."

By 2010, Shankman's side project was drawing revenues of nearly $1 million per year.[1] That year, he sold it to a PR software company (now known as OutMarket) for undisclosed terms. He shuttered his PR firm and, boosted by HARO, launched a career as a full-time author, speaker, and consultant. With a simple, free idea, he provided tremendous value to hundreds of thousands of journalists and marketing professionals. In the process, he built a powerful and loyal following that's enabled him to take his career to the next level.

As a PR specialist, Shankman intimately understood the frustration of journalists who couldn't find the right person to interview for their articles, and companies or individuals desperate to tell their story but unable to find a journalist who was interested. At practically zero cost, he built an e-mail list—an almost ridiculously simple tool that nonetheless reduced inefficiencies in the marketplace and provided a valuable service. In almost every industry, there are gaps. Authors want to be discovered, and agents—overwhelmed by aspirants—want to find the gems. Home buyers want to sell their houses, and prospective new owners want to sift through and find the one that's right for them. Entrepreneurs want start-up capital, and venture capitalists want to find the unicorn-like investment that can return 10x or 100x what they put in. If you can find unique and efficient ways of bringing both sides together and making it easier for them to connect, you can build a powerful community.

Think about the parties you might be able to connect, en masse or individually, and how they could benefit. The author James Altucher writes about the concept of "permission networking"—making a thoughtful connection between two (or sometimes more) people, for a specific reason, and with the permission of both. For instance, if John writes a magazine column about tech start-ups and Mary has just launched an amazing new venture-backed company, it may be a win-win for me to connect them—but only if they both agree first (John may not want to meet anyone now because he's got enough column material for the next six months, and Mary may want to wait on media opportunities because she's assessing an acquisition offer). Reach out to them separately, make the reason for your introduction clear, and see if they're game. If yes, you can proceed with the connection. Making thoughtful connections and introductions helps others, and they'll be appreciative that you were the one to bring them together.

ASK YOURSELF:

- Which people, or types of people, would most benefit from being connected to each other?
- What challenges do they face? What questions do they need answered?
- How can you be helpful to your community? What kinds of assistance would benefit them most?
- How can you help them connect with each other— and you? What's the best method to bring them together (online, in person, via Skype, a combination)?

CREATE A PLATFORM FOR COMMUNITY

Through HARO, Peter Shankman directly matched up parties who wanted to connect with each other (journalists and sources). But what if you could also harness the power of the Internet to create an active community that engaged more broadly with one another? You could help others build relationships, trade best practices, share ideas, and perhaps attract new clients or opportunities.

Scott Belsky, who took design classes in college and hung out with talented, artistic friends, decided that kind of platform was exactly what he wanted to build for the creative community. He admired their visionary ideas—and found it sad and frustrating when, so often, he saw them fail to follow through on that vision. "I realized the likelihood of an idea happening has no correlation to how great the idea is," he says. "But if that's not a factor, what is?"

He suspected it was people's difficulty getting and staying organized, and holding themselves accountable for progress. That's certainly not a problem unique to the creative world, as he discovered when he landed a job at Goldman Sachs after college. Many executives have the same challenges, but there are vastly more resources, from executive coaches to training programs, to help them with it. What could artists or other creative professionals accomplish if they had the same opportunities?

He applied to business school, with a singular focus: helping to organize the creative world. "I remember in my essays saying, 'This is the most disorganized community on the planet and I want to do something about it,'" he says. At Harvard Business School, where most students are dying to get hired by Goldman, the firm he'd just left, he didn't exactly fit in. "I was very misunderstood," he recalls. "I remember Career Services thought I was sick because I hadn't dropped a résumé off [for consulting and investment bank interviews], and everyone else had. There were not a lot of entrepreneurial ventures in 2007 and 2008," when he was in school.

The first product Belsky hoped to offer was a paper-based organizing tool, and that also mystified his classmates. "I think people were like, 'He designed a paper pad he's going to sell? *That's* what he's going to do after business school?'" Undeterred, he relished the chance to work with the creativity expert Professor Teresa Amabile, as well as the focused opportunity to explore his idea. "Business school provided a time where I could get away with playing with it without having to answer to anyone," he says. "I didn't have any investors, I didn't have to explain myself. If it didn't work out a year and a half later, no one would ask me about it. So there was some risk mitigation in exploring the idea that business school afforded."

He made the most of it, commuting each week between Boston and New York, where he was working with two staffers on his start-up. Besides the organizing tool, his company—known as Behance—launched a book series with advice on how creatives can be more effective and productive, an annual conference featuring inspiring speakers, and blog content focused on nitty-gritty questions that bedevil many creative professionals: *How do you know what to charge? When do you fire clients? How do you hire people to help you?* Books, conferences, and paper-based organizers might seem like an unusual mix, but to Belsky, the commonality was clear: "Everything we do is to organize and empower creative people. We use any medium we can to try to achieve this mission."

One feature particularly stood out. Creatives could upload their portfolios to the site, allowing them to get feedback and gain exposure. "Before Behance, everyone had their personal Web site that was discovered by maybe ten people," says Belsky. "No one would have their Web site show up in Google, unless you search for that person's name. A [personal Web site] preaches to the choir, to people who know you." Behance, as the first widely popular portfolio site, became a legitimate discovery vehicle that led to connections and contracts.

Fundamentally, says Belsky, the business is about community. By 2012, the site had grown to more than a million members. Late that year, even Belsky's Harvard Business School classmates had to realize the value of what he'd created, when he sold the company to Adobe for a reported $150 million in cash and stock.[2] He stayed on as vice president of community for Adobe, which is famous for tools like Illustrator and Photoshop that are widely used by creatives. "The initial tenet for Behance was to 'leverage our role in the epicenter of the creative world,'" he says. "And we wrote that at a time when we were *by no means* the epicenter of the creative world. But that's what we aspired to be, and that's the route we took."

Many of us start with a problem we'd like to solve, or a population we'd like to help. For Belsky, it was: *How can artists or other creative professionals better accomplish their vision?* Identify the problem you want to solve, and think about ways you can bring others together so they can connect and learn from one another. It could be online or in the real world. One fun strategy is hosting dinners (or brunches, or cocktail parties) for people you think should meet. For instance, I've started a semiregular dinner series for business authors in the New York City area, which enables them to network with one another, and when I'm traveling to other cities, will often host a meetup for locals who participate in Renaissance Weekend, one of my favorite conferences, which features an eclectic mix of professionals from the worlds of business, politics, and more. You could do the same for any group—connecting "alumni" of a certain company where you used to work, colleagues who all have their own podcasts, or friends who work in the finance industry. Whether it's a Web site, a listserv, or a brunch party, creating a platform for others to connect and engage can dramatically accelerate the pace with which great new ideas can flourish.

ASK YOURSELF:

- What needs or concerns does your peer group or community have? How can you help them (e.g., win publicity, obtain new clients, answer legal questions)? How can you add value to their lives?
- What opportunities can you create, online and off, for your community to connect with one another? How can you spark interaction and conversations?
- What tools can you create to make it easier for them to accomplish their goals? For Belsky, this ranged from a high-tech Web site featuring portfolios to the very low tech (a paper organizer).

CREATE A TRIBE

You've built a following for your idea, and it's begun to spread. Like-minded communities are springing up, and people are connecting because of you. What next? In chapter 5, we talked about Abraham Maslow and his hierarchy of needs; at the top was self-actualization, or fulfilling one's true potential. Later in life, Maslow added another, even higher level: self-transcendence, or going beyond our own individual experience. Self-transcendence can be understood spiritually, but it also reflects a fundamental truth about thought leadership: once you've achieved your own goals, the next—profoundly fulfilling—step is to help teach others how to achieve theirs. It's rare behavior in a world filled with so many constantly striving professionals. But it's one that Seth Godin has embraced. While many popular business authors charge high fees for access to them—and Godin does the same, when it comes to corporate speaking engagements—he has a different policy for his everyday fan base.

He may be unique among top business thinkers in running his own periodic internship programs, including a six-month "alternative MBA" in 2009, in which interns from around the world moved to New York to work with Godin. "I got more out of it than they did," he says, "because the act of sitting with people face-to-face for that long was really powerful for all of us." It's quite likely the interns would have shelled out substantial money for the opportunity to get to know Godin; but as part of his ethos of generosity, he does the opposite and pays them. Three hundred fifty people applied for Godin's program; his acceptance rate was 2.5 percent. For the class of 2015, Harvard Business School's was 12 percent.[3]

Four years later, Godin put out a call for a new crop of

interns. ". . . [A]s usual, there are no guarantees," he wrote. "No guarantees that it will work, or even launch. I can promise that it'll be interesting."[4] That was enough for Tim Walker. A thirty-five-year-old Canadian, he grew up going to a summer camp in Ontario, just an hour north of the one where Godin had once worked—a fact he knew because he was a fanatical reader of Godin's blog. "Life is a bit of an adventure," he says, "and if you have a chance to work with someone who's a hero of yours and get it firsthand, then you do it."

Some might wonder why a thirty-five-year-old would want a summer internship. Isn't that a college thing? But Walker, who had recently sold the digital agency he'd cofounded, was looking for new opportunities. "Part of it is probably generational," he says. "The idea that you're going to learn all the stuff you need to learn at the beginning of your career, and then go have a career, is just a very traditional way of thinking about work and learning. We're now having tons of careers and changing directions, so I think you need to have that mind-set to survive nowadays: that you're going to be constantly learning."

Walker knew the competition would be intense. In fact, the 2013 internship drew more than 3,500 applications. Somehow, he had to stand out and get noticed. "He's shaped so many of my ideas," he says. "It's a great way to learn: get as close to the things that light you up as possible and hope the dots connect after a little while."

He was ready for the challenge. "They say you should research your employer before you apply for a job, that you should know about the company and read their Web site and all that kind of stuff," he says. "Well, it's like I had been doing fifteen years of that [with Godin] before the opportunity arrived. I knew all this stuff about Seth and what he's like and what he appreciates. So it was really just drawing back and thinking about points that I knew would resonate with him." Walker talked about their shared love of camping: "He was big into solo canoeing, and I was like, 'You learn a particular mind-set at summer camp. It's a place of growth and learning, where you help people be their best selves.' I knew he would understand, and I said, 'I'll bring that to your project.'"

Walker also wrote about Project Lifeboat, a volunteer initiative he founded with his partner, Alia McKee, that focuses on providing tools to strengthen friendships. And because Godin was looking for interns with particular business skills, Walker emphasized his role starting and growing Biro, the digital agency he'd sold. When Walker got the nod, he was ecstatic. For two weeks, he moved into a hotel in a small town north of New York City where Godin lives and works. It turns out he wasn't the only nontraditional intern. "This was the most diverse group I had ever hung out with," he says. "The only thing we had in common was that we knew Seth. There was a forty-five-year-old African American lawyer from D.C. There was a woman from Panama who does entrepreneurial education. There were two Ruby on Rails programmers from Brooklyn in their twenties. You name it and that person was there."

Like a good camp counselor, Godin set the tone. Walker recalls, "He's like, 'Here's the thing, here's the idea I have. Let's work it out.' There were no rules that said you had to do something. . . . It was like a Montessori school." One of the best parts of the experience, Walker says, was observing Godin's leadership style up close. "It's this amazing mix of 'We have shit to do and we're going to get it done, and you're not going to be very comfortable because you're going to be pushed out of your limits, and I'm going to be holding you to account and there's no messing around.' And then mixing that with, 'And I'm going to cook all of you lunch every day and tell you wonderful stories to inspire you and show you that it's okay, whatever you're feeling in this situation.'"

Godin took a genuine interest in the interns, Walker recalls. "At one point, the woman from Panama was talking about how fences are a sign of being middle class—that when you've reached out of poverty, you build a fence. And he just stopped the whole thing and said, 'Tell me more about this.' She told him, and he was like, 'I'm a story collector. This is what I do. Everywhere I go, I'm looking for these nuggets that can teach me something and teach other people something in a new way.' You can see his eyes light up: 'Whoa, stop, tell me what goes on in Panama.'"

The project Walker and his compatriots worked on was called Krypton, which created curricula for people to study an idea (such as overcoming fear) and come together to discuss it. The syllabus would include everything from reading book excerpts to blog posts to watching TED talks and reading Wikipedia entries. But Godin's ambitions for the project were much larger than a simple book club. Recalls Walker, "He talked about it to us as, 'We're going to be disrupting the education system. We have to find a new way to learn.'"

The interns built syllabi for ten courses, including ones based around Gretchen Rubin's *The Happiness Project* and Jacqueline Novogratz's *The Blue Sweater* (a memoir about fighting global poverty). "They were really good courses," says Walker. The technology side of the project—creating a platform to help people organize their Krypton courses—didn't go as planned. "It was a disaster," he says. "Everything was happening at the same time, so we were planning [the project] at the same time as the technology people were building it."

The technology glitches didn't dampen Walker's enthusiasm for the project, however. "Sometimes, if you're around your hero and something doesn't work, you're like, 'He's not the person I thought he was.'" But Godin was different from the start. "He didn't build himself up to be perfect. That helps when things go wrong; that's great leadership: 'Failure is okay. We tried things as an experiment, and we do our best.'"

You don't necessarily have to start your own internship program. But are there ways you can become a mentor to others, and connect them not just to you, but to an idea and to one another (the definition of a "tribe" that Godin offers in his popular book *Tribes: We Need You to Lead Us*)? Serving as a mentor can be a powerful way to crystallize your own ideas, give back to others, learn new tricks, and build a base of support for your idea in the world.

Think through who your ideal mentee would be. What kind of person could you help the most? Who would you be most interested in spending time with? If you work at a software company and have great social skills, perhaps you could take young engineers under your wing and help them learn to communicate more effectively. Perhaps you feel called to mentor women or people of color at your company, or you could coach fellow professionals who have lost their jobs and are trying to find their way back into the workforce.

Do you have a ready stream of potential mentees now? If you're a senior partner at a law firm, there are probably tons of young associates who'd be excited to spend more time learning from you. If you're in a position with fewer ready-made opportunities, you can raise your hand to volunteer—perhaps through your local chamber of commerce or professional development group, or spread the word among your friends and colleagues. It's also important to think through what your ideal mentor-mentee relationship would look like, so you can start the connection off right. Perhaps you'd like a short, intensive session like Godin's recent internship program, or you might prefer a lower-impact engagement over time (meeting once a month for breakfast over the course of a year).

Finally, it's worth exploring what you'd like to get out of the connection. This shouldn't be a one-way street, with the mentee receiving all the benefit. Think about what you'd like to learn from them, whether it's getting a Gen Y perspective on the workplace, a peek into new technology trends, or perhaps a cross-cultural experience if you're working with someone from a different background. The sense that you're learning and growing will make the relationship more enjoyable, and also help the mentee feel comfortable that they're also giving value back to you.

Godin, for his part, has cultivated a generation of talent.

Past interns include Ramit Sethi and Harper Reed, chief technology officer for Barack Obama's 2012 reelection campaign and, before that, CTO of the popular online start-up Threadless. His ethos of mentorship has impacted both readers and the people who have worked with him up close. The lasting lesson, says Tim Walker, is that if you have an idea, "it's generous to bring it forward."

ASK YOURSELF:

- What will you do to support and encourage the next generation of talent?
- Could you take on an intern, or group of interns, to help with a project? What would it look like? How could you create a great learning experience—for them and for you?
- Alternatively, would you be interested in interning or apprenticing for someone else? Whom would you choose? What would you like to learn?
- Who would be *your* ideal mentor? How will you get noticed by that person and build a relationship with him or her? How can you add value for him or her as well?

MAKE IT FUN

Finally, as you think about making an impact with your work, it's also essential to ask yourself: how can we create something people can't wait to participate in? These days, we're all too busy. We have too many meetings and obligations; we have to stay late for work; we don't get enough time with our friends and family. The last thing the world needs is another boring initiative with droning conference calls. Too often, we forget that our professional lives can, and should, be joyful. Being bored isn't a sign that something is serious and important; it's a sign that something is seriously wrong. It's possible to share ideas, make connections, build a following—and simultaneously have a blast. Tech start-ups are famous for their perks, from delicious free food to on-site chair massages, which help make people excited to come to work. Charlie Hoehn, author of *Play It Away*, writes about his realization that business meetings are infinitely more enjoyable if you schedule a game of catch with someone instead of just grabbing a coffee. Similarly, if you can find a way to organize something different—and fun— you'll prompt people to *want* to come to your meetings or take part in your initiative. At that point, you stand a very good chance of having your idea go viral, because people want to talk about what excites them. That's the insight that propelled nonprofit fund-raiser Robbie Samuels to his professional success.

Over the years, he'd become frustrated with the silos inside Boston's social justice community. Why weren't the environmentalists talking with the health care advocates, or the LGBT activists talking with the antiracism community? There was plenty to learn from one another. "I was hoping to find other organizers, and we'd get to know and support each other," he recalls. "We'd prevent reinventing the wheel, share best practices, and reinvigorate our work." Everyone liked the idea, but told him they were too busy to participate. "I realized that what we needed was something that wasn't a meeting, wasn't a conference, and wasn't work, and would help us avoid burnout."

He hit on the idea of starting a Meetup group, and called it Socializing for Justice (SoJust). Twice a month, nonprofit advocates and their friends would gather for a purely social event—Bowling for Justice, Cocktails for Justice, Knitting for Justice, and the like. Within six weeks, they were drawing 150 attendees. Part of it was the climate that Samuels and his cofounder, Hilary Allen, sought to create. Participants all wore name tags that also read "I'm looking for" and "Ask me about," which provided easy conversation starters. "Right away, it was about creating a welcoming space and engaging with people," he says. "How could we do something that would help people feel engaged and connected?"

For Samuels, it came down to what he describes as "the difference between inviting and welcoming." Many events invite diverse participants to attend—and then are flummoxed when they either don't show up or fail to return. "As organizers, we host things and talk about who didn't show up," he says. "We hypothesize about where *they* get their information—fill in the blank who 'they' is, though in Boston it's often people of color—and so we post on those Web sites or in that newsletter. But when they show up, they circle the room, no one talks to them, and they leave. We have to make it a priority for all regulars to be welcoming, and that's a cultural shift we've adopted for SoJust."

As soon as you attend three meetings in a relatively short period of time, you're pulled aside. "We remind you about the culture and how welcoming everyone was," says Samuels. Now you're expected to act like a host and be similarly welcoming to others. "The magical part is that if you focus on welcoming everybody, you'll invariably welcome those who need it—demographic outliers, like someone who's older when most people are younger, or people of color in a mostly white environment."

Samuels developed a principle to govern SoJust interactions, charmingly titled "Bagels vs. Croissants." Whereas participants at most other organizations' events huddle into tight circles (like a bagel), making it difficult for outsiders to break into the conversation, SoJusters are exhorted to stand in a semicircle (like a croissant) so they can welcome strangers into the fold. Even the events themselves are intended to encourage mixing and diversity. In the early days of the group, they'd deliberately meet in locations all across the city, from the traditionally black Roxbury to the yuppie haven of Jamaica Plain. "We really didn't want to become pigeonholed at all—we didn't want to be the gay group, or the liberal group, or the environmental group, or the white group," he says. "That was something very intentional."

Over the past eight years, SoJust has grown to more than 2,400 members. People have found job and volunteer opportunities through the network, and developed their professional skills through regular "SkillShare" events, in which an expert presents a low-cost workshop. Samuels believes the networking has helped strengthen the nonprofit community as a whole, but he counts himself as one of the biggest beneficiaries.

He began offering workshops through SoJust, including

"The Art of the Schmooze," his philosophy of how to network in an inclusive fashion. His trainings have become so popular, he's launched a side business providing them for universities and other nonprofits. "There are several trainings I offer on a regular basis for what I think is very good money, and I work with great organizations," he says. "I love teaching and doing trainings and I don't think I would have known where to start if I hadn't had the groundwork [of SoJust]. The platform of SoJust made it easy for me to be seen as an expert, because people saw it was successful and I was in the middle of it."

He's also benefited in other ways. Samuels led a small group discussion at a "Dating While Feminist" meeting held by a partner organization. He met Jess, and invited her to the next SoJust event. "It was Board Games for Justice, and she was good at Scrabble and looking for someone to play with regularly." Today, she's his wife. If it hadn't been for SoJust, "we wouldn't have crossed paths in this big city. We really wouldn't."

Samuels was successful because he realized that if he was going to succeed in bringing people together, it would have to be a social event they actively wanted to attend. In the much-heralded "attention economy," it's more important than ever to ensure that people opt in—that you're creating something so valuable, they choose to seek it out. When Samuels provided the opportunity for tired and overworked nonprofit organizers to connect with like-minded peers, relax, make friends, and have fun, they couldn't resist.

How can you take advantage of the same idea? His target audience probably needed more professional development activities, but that's not what they *wanted*—so he lured them in with Cocktails for Justice, and built a following so robust, it grew to become one of the most important professional development and networking venues in the city. Too often, we think of social change and professional success as deadly serious endeavors. But perhaps we need to ask ourselves how we can bring more fun into everything we do.

Think about the activities you do purely for pleasure. A classic example is taking current or prospective clients out for a golf game, and enjoying beautiful weather and several hours of in-depth conversation with them. But—thankfully for nongolfers like myself—that's not the only way to do it. If you like cooking, think about ways to integrate that into your networking (I sometimes invite business contacts over for spaghetti and my homemade marinara sauce). Could you turn an art opening into a meetup opportunity for professionals who share your interest? How about inviting a group to join you for an author discussion and dinner afterward? Or, if your group gets large or prominent enough, you could even start inviting authors or other business leaders to speak to your organization directly. In a world where the lines of work and your personal life are blurring, you might as well blend networking and your hobbies in order to make them both more fun.

ASK YOURSELF:

■ What would motivate busy people to want to come to your events or join your cause? What's in it for them?

- How can you make your group more inclusive and welcoming to all? What will you do to help others take ownership of the idea or issue and get actively involved?

- How can you make your ideas fun? Set a timer and brainstorm for fifteen minutes.

MAKING IT HAPPEN

YOU'VE DEVELOPED YOUR breakthrough idea, and built a following and community around it. The world is starting to catch on—but before it can take root, you have to ensure that you've set up the systems to make it sustainable. In part 3, we'll discuss how to make the time, and carve out the mental space, necessary to find your ideas and start sharing them with others. We'll also talk about monetization—how to make a living, or at least a decent return on investment, from the work you do. Whether it's writing books, blogging, giving speeches, or selling products, thought leaders employ various strategies, and we'll lay out options for you to consider. Finally, we all know it takes hard work to succeed. But exactly what does that mean? We'll get real and go beyond the rhetoric, looking at exactly what some of the most successful rising stars have done to break through. None of it is easy. But if it's possible for others, with hard work, it's possible for you.

Putting
Thought
Leadership
into Practice

9

I n the course of this book, we've heard from dozens of professionals who have reached the top of their field. They come out of different backgrounds, and have vastly different approaches. Eric Schadt blew open the doors of biology by applying his knowledge of mathematics, while Robbie Samuels created a gathering place for nonprofit activists. Sophal Ear, inspired by his Cambodian heritage, put that country's geopolitics center stage and became a top researcher on areas as diverse as avian flu epidemics and foreign aid policy. Meanwhile, Kare Anderson assembled two intimate groups of colleagues who have helped one another succeed and thrive professionally for more than twenty years.

All these leaders are talented and had great ideas, but sometimes even the best ideas falter in the face of lackluster execution. The thought leaders profiled here all *made it happen.* Despite the pressure of other responsibilities, they made the time to find and develop their ideas, and connect with the people they needed to reach. They took responsibility for finding ways to support themselves—because an idea can't be sustainable if its creator can't survive. Finally, they made the effort—sometimes an extraordinary effort that others can't begin to imagine. But nothing they did was superhuman; it was just focused hard work that anyone, if they're willing to make the sacrifice, can emulate.

MAKING TIME FOR REFLECTION

In a fast-paced society, it's hard to resist the pull of technology, or the elusive goal of in-box zero. *Hold on—I need to check my messages!* We can't help feeling overwhelmed at times. Deadlines loom. E-mails pile up. Speeches need to be written. Some thought leaders even embrace their always-on state as a competitive advantage, but that is a mistake. It turns out that setting aside time for quiet contemplation—even just once in a while—can have a tremendously positive impact on the quality of your ideas.

A while back, when I moderated a tech conference panel discussion and asked about the possibility of social media overload, Robert Scoble responded by holding up the spare battery he carried for his smart phone, to ensure that he never ran out of power. There's no alternative to being constantly engaged, he said: get used to it. He's not alone in embracing the overload; studies have shown that professionals often feel more creative when they're facing time pressures, Harvard Business School professor Teresa Amabile has discovered.[1] (She's the professor that Scott Belsky of Behance sought out as a mentor.)

It turns out that for most people, however, *that feeling is actually an illusion*. "Very high levels of time pressure should be avoided if you want to foster creativity on a consistent basis," Amabile says, because extreme stress hinders the expansive, associative thinking needed for creative insight (and can lead to burnout over time).[2] Similarly, research by Dutch psychologist Ap Dijksterhuis shows that "unconscious thinkers"—people who are temporarily distracted—often make better decisions than "conscious thinkers" who are focused directly on a problem.[3] The panic of a time crunch might eliminate distractions and get you through your to-do lists faster, but the quality of your work might suffer. You don't know what ideas you are missing because your brain doesn't have space for reflection.

One of the best places for creative insight is the shower, where the mindless ritual allows your brain to wander just enough to spark new insights. Early in his career, when Seth Godin was searching for the right language to describe his theory of Internet marketing, he vowed to his team one day that he wasn't going to come in the next day until he'd found a name for his idea, "even if I have to spend an hour in the shower." It worked, and he coined the now-famous term "permission marketing," the title of his popular 1999 book. "Once we had the words, it became easy," he says. "I wrote the book in six weeks."

Rose Shuman, too, was in a contemplative frame of mind when the idea for Question Box came to her. Thinking about a public call box, she wondered: what if a similar device could help connect people to the Internet? She was open enough to her surroundings to take in inspiration from what was around her. For four hours, notebook in hand, she had what she describes as a "musing session." Even Daniel Goleman of *Emotional Intelligence* fame stumbled upon the idea by reading a journal article—an activity that, in today's deadline-driven world, might even be called "leisurely." The Internet wasn't in widespread use back then; he wasn't clicking links to see the latest headlines or cat videos. Instead, he was digging deep and looking for new ideas.

Building time into your life for reflection is easier said than done. Many of us have tried (and failed) to set up a morning meditation routine, or have subscribed to thought-provoking magazines only to see them heaped in a pile on our desks or appear as a foreboding cascade of unread tiles on our tablets. Creating the space for quiet thought and self-care might seem unproductive, but giving yourself room to think may be your greatest competitive advantage in an increasingly frenzied world. While everyone else is reacting, you can make thoughtful, considered decisions. While everyone else is chasing the latest fad, you can look at the big picture and see where the future is going.

What systems do you have in place to ensure that you can recharge and think? Each day, it could be a fifteen-minute walk after lunch. Each week, it could be a couple of hours blocked out on your schedule to muse about big-picture strategy. Each month, it could be a morning spent with your mastermind group. And each year, it could be a "reading vacation," as popularized by Bill Gates, who finds inspiration by binge-reading his way through a stack. Whatever your preferred method, find some way to give your mind the space it needs to come up with (or further develop) your breakthrough idea.

ASK YOURSELF:

- What activities make you feel most energized or creative (exercise, meditation, brainstorming with a journal, etc.)?
- How can you build time into your schedule for that reflection? Take your calendar and start by blocking out one hour in the next week simply to think.
- What strategies will you use to tap the power of unconscious thought? Instead of sitting at your desk and pounding away at a problem, go to the gym or take a shower.
- What are you missing? At least once a day when you're out of your house or the office, make a point of noticing your surroundings. What do you see? What objects or concepts could illuminate your situation?
- What should you be reading? Make a list of newspapers, magazines, or journals you want to read regularly. Buy a subscription and make time on your calendar. Whether you read them on the exercise bike, while you're eating lunch, or just before bed, make a point to do it.
- When can you "turn off" temporarily? Even the simple act of turning off your smart phone during dinner can help you engage better in the present moment.

MAKING TIME FOR LUCK

There's something else that the best thinkers make time for in their schedules: luck. It may sound crazy to suggest you can control luck, but if you think about it, most of us—the overscheduled masses—have engineered it *out* of our lives, and it's time to fix that. "Just look at your calendar," says John Hagel of Deloitte's Center for the Edge. "How tightly scheduled are you? Have you got a breakfast meeting, meetings all day, then late night meetings? There's not much chance for serendipity there unless a fire alarm goes off and you have to head into the street. Create spaces where you're wandering around and exposing yourself to new people."[4]

What does it look like to make time for luck in your life? As Anthony Tjan, coauthor of *Heart, Smarts, Guts, and Luck: What It Takes to Be an Entrepreneur and Build a Great Business,* told me, "Luck is often mislabeled in business."[5] It's not so much that people are lucky, but that they're interested in other people and aren't rushing along to the next, better thing. As Tjan notes, "Lucky people have an openness, an authenticity, and a generosity toward embracing people—without overthinking 'what's the value exchange?' It's just, *that's an interesting person.* It might be someone working in a restaurant, someone in an unrelated industry, or a taxi driver, and ten years later when that person becomes somehow critical, people say, *that's so lucky—they happened to meet someone in college, or they were on the same boat with them.*"

When we're too deliberate and focused on building our

network, we often get tunnel vision. "There are plenty of times when you're going to conferences or cocktail parties, and you're thinking about where there's a fit [in making a connection]," says Tjan. "You're trying to quickly assess and screen value, and we all fall prey to that." Unfortunately, that means you may overlook anyone who deviates from the stereotype of what a great leader or rising professional "should" look like. You may miss the shy entrepreneur hiding in the corner, or the guy wearing nerdy clothes who turns out to be an influential blogger.

People who self-identify as "lucky"—and are therefore perhaps a little more laid-back and open to chance—"are the ones who discover the wallflowers," says Tjan, "and they benefit disproportionately later in life from some of those relationships." While it's critical to work hard and make your own opportunities, it pays to recognize that we don't have to control everything in life. Leave room in your schedule for the unexpected—the colleague popping by your office with an interesting idea, or the chance to take a surprise call from an old friend you haven't spoken with in ages. If you're too Type A to even know where to begin, you can follow the lead of one self-described "lucky" person interviewed by psychologist Richard Wiseman, who revealed that in order to force himself to diversify the types of people he talked to, he would attend an event and approach only people wearing a particular color. If your network is too heavy with fellow marketers, or thirty-something tech guys, or mom entrepreneurs, make it a point to attend events that attract a wide cross section—and avoid clustering in homogeneous groups by using the "colored shirt" strategy.

Part of it is just keeping your eyes open and being alert to your surroundings. A while back, I was having dinner by myself in a restaurant in Cambridge, Massachusetts. I was engrossed in my newspaper and wasn't paying much attention, when someone called my name. It took me a moment to place him, and for good reason: I had met Cory six months earlier, across the country at a conference in Napa Valley. He lived in Washington, D.C., and was visiting Boston for only a couple of days.

I was astonished he'd recognized me and that we'd run into each other in such a random venue. But he wasn't surprised at all. "I grew up in a small town," he told me. "I'm used to recognizing people everywhere I go." I'd lived in the Boston area for many years, and had grown accustomed to being surrounded by strangers; I rarely even bothered to scan the room for people I might know. But Cory carried his small-town attitude around the world with him; he *expected* to recognize people, and, because he was looking, he was often proved right. It was lucky that we ran into each other, but—because of Cory's worldview and approach to life—it wasn't really luck at all.

ASK YOURSELF:

- How can you bring more serendipity into your life? Start by paring back your schedule and leaving room for the unexpected. Make it a rule to leave at least one hour unscheduled per day, to allow room for emergencies—or lucky opportunities.
- How can you meet people you normally wouldn't come across? At the next conference you attend,

make a point of seeking out and striking up conversations with people who are wearing green (or red or purple) that day.

■ Are you overthinking the value exchange? Learn to step back and appreciate people for who they are, rather than immediately wondering how they can help you or if the conversation is a "good use of your time."

MAKING A LIVING

You may be in the fortunate position of being able to develop expert content and build your community as part of your "day job," with a guaranteed salary to fall back on. Alternatively, you may see thought leadership as a fulfilling hobby that complements your full-time work. That worked for years for Michael Waxenberg, who pursued his real estate avocation first as an unpaid reviewer, and later as a part-time Realtor. Throughout, he kept his family anchored with the salary from his full-time work in IT.

Unfortunately, for many aspiring thought leaders seeking to make a living from their work, it would be easy to devote all their time to writing free online articles, helping others tremendously, and building a powerful reputation— all while starving. It's important to recognize that being generous doesn't mean being a martyr to your cause, or that you can't be generous to yourself. Just as artists are increasingly turning to their fans to fund Kickstarter campaigns for their next movie or album, it's entirely appropriate for professionals of all stripes to look to their community to help support the valuable work they're providing. Some monetize through speaking, coaching, or online products, and still others have sold companies they created or turned their passions into full-time paid positions. There's no clear template to becoming a recognized expert in your field, which means there's no clear template for how to support yourself as one. Many thinkers profiled in this book take a smorgasbord approach, earning funds in a variety of different ways. Based on your personality and interests, you can find the right strategy for you.

Seth Godin, who is committed to blogging for free and funding generous internship programs, isn't afraid to ask for money where it counts. "I've made a choice that there are two kinds of work I do," he says. The first, he says, is "when someone wants me to give a speech or something like that, and I charge a lot of money to do that." Accepting a high speaking fee allows him the luxury to do the second kind of work—his pro bono passions that enable him to give back.

Alan Weiss also earns money from professional speaking, but the core of his business today centers on teaching others the skills he's learned in more than thirty years as a solo consultant. He started his career working with large corporate clients. But after the publication of his 1992 best seller *Million Dollar Consulting*, detailing how to create a seven-figure consulting practice, a slew of aspirants began reaching out: could they meet him for coffee or schedule a call to pick his brain? "At first, I was flattered," says Weiss. "But I began spending more time giving advice than with clients, so I decided to charge for it. I thought people would demur, and then I'd have a good excuse [not to speak with them for free]. Even my wife said, 'I don't think anyone will pay you for advice.'"

It was 1996, and he named a deliberately high price for individuals—$3,500 for six months' access to his "mentor program." (With inflation, the equivalent in 2014 would have been $5,300.) He describes the program as "the equivalent of being on retainer for a corporation. You're a sounding board, you provide feedback, and people come to you for advice on a given matter. You might role-play a scenario, critique a proposal, or debrief on what's happened." He came up with the number because it was the cost of a monthly lease for a Ferrari, and figured if twelve people agreed, he could have the car for free. To his surprise, far more than a dozen people took him up on it.[6]

He continued the program for nearly fifteen years, at which point he launched two variations—an intensive nine-month coaching program priced at $17,000, and his "Master Mentor" program, in which he certifies existing members of his mentor program (for a fee of $10,000) to take on their own mentees. They'll retain access to Weiss and be able to call for advice, and he gets a cut of the proceeds for each initial enrollment. (If the mentee re-ups, all subsequent fees go to the Master Mentor.) He even offers a $55,000 "Alan Card," a prepurchase deal that entitles bearers to a 30 percent discount on his workshops, access to his videos and teleconferences, and two half-day sessions and dinner with him.[7]

By late 2013, between the mentor and the Master Mentor programs, Weiss estimated that he had worked with approximately two thousand people. The aspiring consultants value their interactions with him, given his powerful brand and demonstrated expertise (he's a prolific author and blogger). Indeed, his high prices—he charges far more than most professional development programs for consultants—actually contribute to the perceived value. As Robert Cialdini told me when I interviewed him for my *Forbes* blog, in "markets in which people are not completely sure of how to assess quality, they use price as a stand-in for quality."[8] You can't compare consulting advice in an apples-to-apples way, as you could with cereal or paper towels. Weiss's high prices reinforce his brand as an elite provider.

Weiss has clearly taken to monetization with gusto, but for many others—especially those who started out by providing content for free—it can be a fraught transition. Some professionals worry that making money through the communities they've built is somehow wrong, immoral, or "selling out"—or, at least, will be perceived that way by others. That was the case for Ramit Sethi when he began to sell online products through his Web site. "It was a very emotionally taxing time when I first started to monetize," he recalls. "It was honestly the scariest thing I've done in my business. I had been writing since 2004—I wrote for free, multiple times a week for three years." He was making no money; there weren't even ads on his Web site.

So in December 2006, he began to wonder: if he sold a product, would anyone buy it? He put together an e-book that he sold for $4.95, which he describes as "a very scary price" at the time. "I have not been that nervous since," he says. The blowback was intense. "People said, 'This site has jumped the shark,' and 'You're a sellout,' and 'So this is *I'll*

Teach Ramit to Be Rich.' I have to tell you, it really hurt. It hurt because I had been giving away my best material, holding nothing back for years. I had helped countless people. I answered e-mails for free."

He estimates he received about fifty to a hundred complaints—not a huge amount given the fifty thousand to seventy-five thousand people who read his blog each month at the time, but enough for him to take notice. He didn't give up on his efforts to make a living from his work, however: "Over the next three years, I realized that what happened that day was that a loud, vocal minority—who never wants to pay—were yelling." He kept experimenting, and as he created more products at higher price points, he learned how to talk about who the product was, and wasn't, right for.

Some people won't want to pay anything for your work—much less what it's actually worth. Ignore them, says Sethi. Five years later, he offered a course for $12,000 and received only ten complaints out of more than a million people who saw it advertised. "I learned how to communicate the value," he says. "The right people love it because in this world, you're not trying to appeal to everyone. You're just trying to get the right people. That's been a transformative lesson I've learned."

Financial success probably won't come overnight. It's rare that you can immediately make a living from your thought leadership. As with Sethi, it may take years to build your audience and get comfortable monetizing—and that's okay, as long as it's part of a deliberate strategy to make enough money to allow you to keep pursuing your dreams over time. When I first started blogging, I wrote for tiny publications for free, just to build up clips and get my name known. I worked my way up to writing for more prominent publications, such as *Harvard Business Review* and *Huffington Post*, also for free.

Now, four years after I started writing regularly, the vast majority of my blogging is paid, providing me with an income that nearly matches what I earned as a rookie reporter fifteen years ago. That may not sound too impressive, but—crucially—it's only a small fraction of the overall revenue I take in. I earn a robust six-figure income from speaking, consulting, coaching, and teaching executive education at top business schools—all activities made possible by the connections and brand equity that my writing helps to create.

It's also essential to be flexible; the way you end up making money may not be the way you initially envisioned. That was the case for Eve Bridburg. She'd just finished her master of fine arts program, and emerged completely demoralized. "It was a very rigorous program, but it felt like the criticism was often kind of mocking," she recalls. "If you want people to do their best writing, they have to feel really safe, take risks, be naked, bare all, and if you're in an environment where you could be mocked, it's not as helpful—or if you feel your fellow students are competing with you, rather than being there to help you."

Even the idea of grading creative writing rankled her. As a graduate teaching fellow, she was forced to. "But it felt weird, it felt wrong," she recalls. "Just when someone was getting it and going deeper, mining for what they were trying to say, you had to put a grade on it. It never felt particularly useful or good to be giving grades on creative work that way."

Along with a friend, Julie Rold, she dreamed up a new

vision—"a piece of it elevated and a piece of it totally self-ish," she says. What if they could create a writing program on their own terms? So in the spring of 1997, she launched GrubStreet, which sought to "bring the rigor of the university into the community, and without grades. We hung up some flyers and taught two classes, and between us, we attracted eight students."

Her group was based in Boston, but the name came from London's Grub Street, the famed home of literary hacks. "They were kind of looked down upon," says Bridburg. Teaching writing outside of a university setting, she could relate. But the response from students was positive, and enrollment rapidly grew. "Part of the success came from hiring teachers who understood the fine line between rigor and love," she says, "and we held tight to that philosophy. Rigorous but supportive: that concept really resonated for people."

GrubStreet started as a for-profit business, but the economics were challenging. Bridburg tried to pay her instructors fairly, and hated to turn aspiring writers away for lack of funds, so profits were slim. "I quickly discovered I was building a community more than a viable business," she recalls. With a small child at home, Bridburg took it as a sign to step back when she discovered she was pregnant again in 2001. Despite GrubStreet's having twenty core instructors and five hundred students, however, no one else wanted to run a business that was only marginally profitable. For a while it seemed the only answer was to shut it down—a depressing realization.

Bridburg made a decision that secured GrubStreet's future, turning it into a nonprofit. She thought she could pull off the transition in a year, and volunteered her time to do so. It actually took four years, but she succeeded in building a secure and viable institution. In 2005, she left GrubStreet to become a literary agent and learn about the other side of the publishing industry. "Getting the founder out of the way is a really healthy thing for an organization because other people step up and make it their own, and that really happened," she says. In 2010, she returned to the organization as its executive director, energized by her stint away, and has been running GrubStreet ever since. By 2012, it was serving more than 2,500 students per year.

Bridburg started by creating the kind of program she wished she'd had. In the process, she's built a literary ecosystem for thousands of Boston writers, giving them employment, networking opportunities, the chance to enhance their craft—and, just maybe, to make a living at it. But it's the sense of community that she, and others, find most valuable. It's "a great asset in an increasingly fragmented publishing landscape," she notes, and students and instructors often buy one another's books and turn out for readings. But even more than that, it's an oasis in a world that often doesn't understand what they're trying to accomplish. "The world is full of people who say, 'Why are you writing?'" she says. "It's seen as narcissistic and a waste of time. But GrubStreet is a group of people who understand its value, cheerlead for you, and help you reach your goals."

Sometimes our long-term vision is exactly right: she knew what was missing in the city, and how to create it. But the particulars may turn out differently from what we imagine. Bridburg didn't set out to become a nonprofit founder, but when she realized that was the best way to keep Grub-

Street alive, she made the transition and has built a lasting institution (in the process, she's even been named one of *Boston* magazine's "50 Most Powerful Women"). It wasn't precisely how she envisioned making money, but her adaptability means she's spent nearly two decades doing the work she loves and helping others thrive.

Take time to research how the thought leaders you admire support themselves. Most provide a mix of products and services; you should think of their offerings as a sample menu from which to glean inspiration. What opportunities feel most interesting, or most comfortable, to you? When I launched my business in 2006, all my income came from **consulting services**; I worked with businesses and nonprofits to help them develop marketing and social media strategies. In 2010, I started to **teach executive education**, at first with one program and later with a half dozen different business schools around the world. By the following year, I finally started to earn money from my **writing**—first, with paid blogging opportunities, and then with a book deal. Around the time my first book, *Reinventing You*, came out in 2013, I'd built up enough of a brand that companies and associations started to pay me to give **speeches**. Finally, by 2014, my book had gained enough momentum that a stream of professionals were approaching me about **executive coaching**. At first, I turned them down, but eventually decided to offer that service to a small number of clients. That's five different business models right there; each business thinker has a different mix.

You may also want to think about **product creation** (can you develop a workbook or program you could sell online?).

You could develop a course or series of **courses** (could you bring together a group of students, in person or online, to learn about a specific topic?). If your audience becomes large enough, **sponsorships** may become a possibility (could you get a company to underwrite your talks or Web site, or use you as a spokesperson?). You may even be able to find a **day job** that aligns perfectly with your thought leadership goals, whether it's working as a professor, a partner at a consulting firm, or an "ambassador" at a corporation.

There's no one right way to make a living from your thought leadership. But you do need to develop a viable business model in some fashion. If you have a trust fund and can afford to run a charitable operation indefinitely, that's a fantastic blessing. But most of us need to make money, and if you consistently behave in ways that aren't financially prudent—like creating content for free, forever—you'll eventually have to give it up when reality intrudes and you need to pay that mortgage or tuition bill. Money certainly isn't everything, but, at a basic level, it's fuel that makes your vision possible. Recognizing its importance and thinking strategically about how to bring in the revenue you need is critical to making your idea sustainable over time.

ASK YOURSELF:

- How can you best communicate the value of your work? Who would be most receptive to that message?
- What can you start doing now, for free, that will eventually lead to paid work? What's your strategy for converting those opportunities into revenue over time?

- Do you feel confident enough to start monetizing? If you're concerned that you don't deserve it, or worry that you're selling out, that ambivalence will come through to others and you won't be successful. Reach out to successful, trusted colleagues for a reality check. Are your concerns justified, or are you holding yourself back?
- Can you segment your work so that some parts are expensive and other parts are free or low cost (ensuring that people of different means can access your ideas, and helping you expand your audience for the future)?
- Are you charging enough for your work? Remember that in many contexts, price creates the perception of quality.

MAKING THE EFFORT

We all know hard work is mandatory for success, but sometimes it's difficult to conceptualize what that actually looks like. Here's a hint: the top performers *exponentially* outwork everyone else. "When entrepreneurs and small business people tell me about their day and they're home by 7, I laugh," author and social media consultant Gary Vaynerchuk told me during an interview for my *Forbes* blog.[9] At the time we spoke, Twitter had recently introduced Vine, its six-second video application, and Vaynerchuk was fascinated by its potential marketing implications. For the past week, he told me, he'd been going to bed between three and four A.M. because he was staying up late to learn about it.

That same principle applies to Daniel Pink, who invests a significant chunk of "marketing" time in one area where many people—who are far less prominent—fail utterly. "On a tactical level, it's insane," he admits. "But I answer every e-mail from readers myself. I put my e-mail address on every book jacket and my Web site. There's even a line encouraging people to e-mail me, and I always answer every single one. If someone has spent twenty-five dollars and devoted five or six hours of their life to something I created, I can spend five minutes answering their e-mail." That personal attention has helped Pink build a passionate fan base that vaults him to the top of the best-seller charts almost as soon as his books are announced.

Tom Peters also built his brand through massive effort. In the months and years following the publication of *In Search of Excellence*, he recalls, "I wasn't getting much sleep, and I was writing articles for anybody and everybody. It was pure brute force. I was doing 125 speeches a year." That may sound punishing—and it is—but it's also liberating. The vast majority of people will never be willing to make the sacrifices necessary to get to the top. They want it handed to them—as Seth Godin says, to be picked by Oprah. If success were determined by what happened to you, you would be stuck if you were not born to genius or privilege. Fortunately, it's often a matter of outworking everyone else. You don't have to be a genius, and you don't even have to be lucky (though we've discussed how to make more time in your schedule for that, too). You just have to want it badly enough.

Angela Lussier, a marketing consultant and career coach, is an example of someone who also launched her career through pure brute force. In 2009, she was working for a recruiting firm, growing more and more frustrated by the day. The candidates she spoke with would often highlight the wrong parts of their résumés, or would otherwise fail to convey their strengths, so she started coaching them. Her bosses were furious, because she'd take too long on each phone call; she wasn't being paid to be a career coach. But, she came to realize, that's exactly what she wanted to do. In April 2009, she walked out the door and started her own business. She knew it was the right decision, but her economic situation was precarious: she only had $2,000 in the bank. "I had to act fast to build this thing," she says.

She reached out to all the local college career centers offering to do free workshops. She figured they might be interested in a former recruiter who wanted to provide career tips for graduating seniors, but most of them didn't even return her messages. She shifted her focus to pitching local libraries on her workshops. "One person said, 'How long have you been in business?' I said, 'Since Monday.'" Not surprisingly, they weren't interested.

With bills to pay, however, she didn't have a choice: She had to keep dialing. After she'd called nearly thirty libraries in her region and been rejected by all of them, one finally said yes. When they asked how many workshops Lussier wanted to offer, she immediately realized she could leverage it into a series. So—without any materials developed—she announced she'd do eight. The librarian followed up: "Can you do one series in the afternoon for people who are unemployed, and another at night for people who have a job?" Lussier quickly agreed. This library gig "was the only credibility I had," she recalls, so she used it to call back other libraries and say, "Northampton is doing this, do you want to do it?" She landed workshop series at two other libraries, and within a week had booked thirty-two workshops over the next two months.

She was excited but alarmed: she had a massive amount of content to create from scratch. Driven by necessity, she created her agenda and worksheets for participants. As she'd hoped, her marketing efforts paid off. "People started coming up to me and saying, *'I want to hire you.'* The phone started ringing, *'Hey, can you do a workshop for us?'*" Almost every day—and sometimes up to three times a day—she did workshops for an eclectic array of groups, from middle schools to Rotary Clubs, and from colleges to women's business groups. "Over the first year I did probably five hundred workshops," recalls Lussier, "and that was how I built my whole business."

Her feat was particularly impressive because public speaking was her greatest fear. She recalls sweating, stuttering, and turning red in front of early audiences. "I realized the most successful people were the communicators," she says, "and if you don't speak up, no one knows what you have to offer and you'll be left behind. I made a promise to myself that I'd learn to speak." She joined Toastmasters and willed herself to practice and improve. More than five hundred talks later—including the panel discussion where I met her—she's certainly arrived.

Are you willing to stay up until four o'clock in the morning to master a new technology? Or give three free workshops a day? The effort that people like Peters, Pink, Vaynerchuk, and Lussier exert is stunning. Their results speak for themselves; they've all built thriving businesses and become recognized experts.

Where can you get the greatest leverage by working hard? Vaynerchuk made his name through online video (he created the popular video blog *Wine Library TV*), so it was a natural extension for him to focus on Vine, a new type of short-form online video. Lussier took a different approach, recognizing that communication skills are central to any successful professional. Because she didn't feel confident speaking up, she decided to face her fears head-on and keep speaking until it came naturally to her. Whether you decide to play to your strengths or try to improve your weaknesses, working harder than everyone else almost always pays off. (In K. Anders Ericsson's much-cited "ten thousand hours" study of professional expertise, by age twenty, the very best violinists had practiced six thousand hours more than their less accomplished peers.[10])

You started with an idea—an idea you identified, developed, and believed in. You tested it with trusted colleagues, shared it with the world, and enabled a community of adherents to make it their own. But for the impact to last—for the idea to spread as far as it can, and help others as much as it can—your work has to be sustainable. You need space to think and reflect and make new connections. You need to be able to earn a good living, so you can focus on the idea and not on unpaid bills or financial concerns. And most of all, you need to be willing to put in the effort, day after day. Most people don't speak up, and never share their ideas with the world. They wait for lightning to strike, without realizing that these possibilities are open to anyone who is willing to do the work. If you believe in your vision, now is the time to act. The world needs your voice.

ASK YOURSELF:

- Where will you "go deep" in your hard work? You can't excel in every area. Gary Vaynerchuk researched social media channels obsessively, and Tom Peters gave multiple speeches per week. What will you emphasize?

- What's holding you back? Angela Lussier knew she couldn't succeed as long as she was afraid of speaking, so she joined Toastmasters and got the help she needed. What are you afraid of, and how will you overcome it?

- What are you going to do *today* to get started? It's easy to come up with ideas and make amorphous future plans. But what are you going to do *right now* to start finding your breakthrough idea, honing it, and bringing it to the world? Good luck, and congratulations.

Classroom or Book Group Discussion Questions

- Who are the thought leaders you admire most, and why? How did you learn about them? How do they share their ideas with the world (blogging, writing books, speaking, etc.)?
- What are the ideas or concepts you're most excited about right now? What intrigues you about them?
- Are there areas in your life where you feel a sense of mission or purpose? Which ones, and why?
- How do you make time for reflection in your life, and find the space to think? What's worked for you and what hasn't?
- Are there areas where you currently feel you have expertise? Which ones? How did you develop that expertise?
- Are you currently sharing that expertise with others? If yes, how? If not, why not?

- Do you have a "mastermind group" of colleagues with whom you share ideas? If yes, what role do they play in your life, and how did you come to be part of the group? If no, are there other ways you're getting professional support and feedback? How could you build more of this into your life?

- Are you currently active on social media? Why or why not? Which channels are most appealing to you, and why? What types of things do you communicate about? How has it benefited or influenced you?

- Are you part of any communities built around an idea (anything from Lean Startup Meetups to religious groups to attending TED or TEDx talks)? If yes, why did the idea speak to you, and what do you get out of your involvement in the community?

ACKNOWLEDGMENTS

Stand Out has been a team effort, and I'm grateful to the many people who have helped make it a reality. Thank you to my agent, Carol Franco, who helped place it in the capable hands of Niki Papadopoulos and Bria Sandford, my editors at Portfolio. Their insights have made *Stand Out* better and hopefully even more useful and inspiring for readers. I'm also grateful to the rest of the Portfolio team, including publisher Adrian Zackheim; production editor Kate Griggs; and the marketing and publicity maestros Will Weisser, Taylor Fleming, and Kathy Daneman, who have worked hard to ensure the message reaches as many people as possible.

My colleague Andy Molinsky of Brandeis University generously shared research insights with me, and my virtual assistants Sue Williams and later Alex D'Amore provided valuable help throughout the writing process.

The professionals interviewed in *Stand Out* are at the top of their fields and are much in demand, but nonetheless made time to speak with me and share their wisdom so that others might learn from their experiences. I truly appreciate their help.

I began developing many of the ideas in *Stand Out* through my writing for publications including *Harvard Business Review,*

Forbes, Entrepreneur, and *AMEX OPEN Forum.* I also give keynote talks and workshops about these concepts frequently, and teach in a number of top business schools. For those who have given me the chance to share and develop these ideas, I'm grateful.

No book is possible, of course, without the love and encouragement of the people closest to you. My mother, Gail Clark, is my most loyal supporter and the person who gave me the confidence to try anything. Ann Thomas helped raise me with love and care. Joel Gagne, to whom this book is dedicated, is the kind of friend everyone deserves but too few people are lucky enough to have in their lives. My cat Gideon, who passed away shortly after I signed the deal for this book, was an amazing force for good during the sixteen years we spent together. Pets teach us about unconditional love in a way that humans simply can't. I hope everyone will consider bringing a homeless pet into their lives (www.petfinder.com). To Gideon, Harriet, and Patty Adelsberger: you are always in my thoughts and I miss you.

NOTES

INTRODUCTION

1. Shel Israel, "What Makes a Thought Leader?" *Forbes*, March 5, 2012. http://www.forbes.com/sites/shelisrael/2012/03/05/what -makes-a-thought-leader.
2. Sarah Green, "The Perils of Self-Promotion," *Harvard Business Review*, January/February 2014. http://hbr.org/2014/01/the -perils-of-self-promotion/ar/1.
3. Drew Desilver, "U.S. Income Inequality, on Rise for Decades, Is Now Highest Since 1928," Pew Research Center, December 5, 2013. http://www.pewresearch.org/fact-tank/2013/12/05/u-s-income -inequality-on-rise-for-decades-is-now-highest-since-1928.
4. This is a topic explored in the athletic world in David Epstein's *The Sports Gene: Inside the Science of Extraordinary Athletic Performance* (Current, 2013).
5. Emmanuel Saez, "Striking It Richer: The Evolution of Top Incomes in the United States," UC Berkeley, September 3, 2013. http://elsa.berkeley.edu/~saez/saez-UStopincomes-2012.pdf.

PART I: FINDING YOUR BREAKTHROUGH IDEA

1. "ISBN Output 2002–2013," chart, Bowker, 2013. http://www .bowker.com/assets/downloads/products/isbn_output_2002_2013 .pdf.
2. "Statistics," YouTube, 2014. https://www.youtube.com/yt/press/ statistics.html.
3. "Twitter Usage Statistics," *Internet Live Stats*, 2014. http://www .internetlivestats.com/twitter-statistics.

CHAPTER 1: THE BIG IDEA

1. Pamela Weintraub, "The Dr. Who Drank Infectious Broth, Gave Himself an Ulcer, and Solved a Medical Mystery," *Discover*, April 8,

2010. http://discovermagazine.com/2010/mar/07-dr-drank-broth
-gave-ulcer-solved-medical-mystery.

2. Dorie Clark, "Competitive Advantage Is Dead: Here's What to Do
   About It," *Forbes*, May 16, 2013. http://www.forbes.com/sites/
   dorieclark/2013/05/16/competitive-advantage-is-dead-heres
   -what-to-do-about-it.
3. "Rita McGrath," Thinkers50, 2014. http://www.thinkers50.com/
   biographies/rita-mcgrath.
4. "Geoarbitrage," *The Blog of Author Tim Ferriss, 2007–2009*. http:
   //fourhourworkweek.com/category/geoarbitrage.
5. Dorie Clark, "How to Become a Top Business Thinker," *Forbes*, July
   21, 2014. http://www.forbes.com/sites/dorieclark/2014/07/21/
   how-to-become-a-top-business-thinker/.

CHAPTER 2: DEVELOP YOUR EXPERT NICHE

1. Adam Sternbergh, "The Spreadsheet Psychic," *New York*, October
   12, 2008. http://nymag.com/news/features/51170/index3.html.
2. Megan Garber, "Nate Silver and *The New York Times*: The Origin
   Story," *The Atlantic*, November 6, 2012. http://www.theatlantic.com/
   technology/archive/2012/11/nate-silver-and-the-new-york-times-the
   -origin-story/264638.
3. Boris Groysberg and Kerry Herman, "Rachael Ray: Cooking Up a
   Brand," *Harvard Business Review*, August 19, 2008. http://hbr.org/
   product/rachael-ray-cooking-up-a-brand/an/409011-PDF-ENG?
   Ntt=409011-PDF-ENG.
4. I highly recommend the *Harvard Business Review* case study above,
   where I first learned Ray's story through guest lecturing for Boris
   Groysberg's class. The fascinating case study inspired me to write a
   blog post for *Harvard Business Review* called "Build Your
   Reputation the Rachael Ray Way." http://blogs.hbr.org/2012/11/
   build-your-reputation-the-r/.
5. Laura Jacobs, "Just Say Yum-O!" *Vanity Fair*, September 11, 2007.
   http://www.vanityfair.com/fame/features/2007/10/
   rachaelray200710, via HBR case study, http://hbr.org/product/
   rachael-ray-cooking-up-a-brand/an/409011-PDF-ENG?Ntt=409011
   -PDF-ENG.
6. Michael Hastings, "Fixing It Fast," *Winston-Salem Journal*, January 1,
   2003, via HBR case study, http://hbr.org/product/rachael-ray-
   cooking-up-a-brand/an/409011-PDF-ENG?Ntt=409011-PDF-ENG.
7. Walter Frick, "Nate Silver on Finding a Mentor, Teaching Yourself
   Statistics, and Not Settling in Your Career," *Harvard Business
   Review*, September 24, 2013. http://blogs.hbr.org/2013/09/nate
   -silver-on-finding-a-mentor-teaching-yourself-statistics-and-not
   -settling-in-your-career.

CHAPTER 3: PROVIDE NEW RESEARCH

1. Al Jones, "Kalamazoo Native Robin Liss Sells Web-tech Cluster to *USA Today*," Michigan Live, February 1, 2011. http://www.mlive.com/business/west-michigan/index.ssf/2011/02/kalamazoo_native_robin_liss_se.html.

CHAPTER 4: COMBINE IDEAS

1. Michael Michalko, "Janusian Thinking," The Creativity Post, June 12, 2012. http://www.creativitypost.com/create/janusian_thinking.
2. "The World's Most Influential Scientific Minds: 2014," Thomson Reuters, June 18, 2014. http://thomsonreuters.com/articles/2014/worlds-most-influential-scientific-minds-2014.
3. Dorie Clark, "How to Win the Talent War," *Huffington Post*, November 15, 2011. http://www.huffingtonpost.com/dorie-clark/how-to-win-the-talent-war_b_1089874.html.

CHAPTER 5: CREATE A FRAMEWORK

1. John Forester, "Fight for Your Right to Cycle Properly!" JohnForester.com, December 12, 2013. http://www.johnforester.com.

CHAPTER 6: BUILD YOUR NETWORK

1. Tim Ferriss, "Tim Ferriss Rethinks Email," Four Hour Workweek, August 5, 2014. http://fourhourworkweek.com/2014/08/05/timothy-ferriss-email.
2. Dorie Clark, "How Mike Michalowicz Went from Unknown, Self-Published Author to Mainstream Publishing Success," *Forbes*, June 4, 2013. http://www.forbes.com/sites/dorieclark/2013/06/04/how-mike-michalowicz-went-from-unknown-self-published-author-to-mainstream-publishing-success.
3. Dorie Clark, "Five Ways to Become a Better Team Player," *Forbes*, March 28, 2012. http://www.forbes.com/sites/dorieclark/2012/03/28/five-ways-to-become-a-better-team-player.
4. Dorie Clark, "How to Get Someone to Like You Immediately," *Forbes*, August 15, 2012. http://www.forbes.com/sites/dorieclark/2012/08/15/how-to-get-someone-to-like-you-immediately.
5. Matthew Bidwell, Shinjae Won, Roxana Barbulescu, and Ethan Mollick, "I Used to Work at Goldman Sachs!: How Organizational Status Creates Rents in the Market for Human Capital," *Strategic Management Journal*, conditionally accepted (2013). http://works.bepress.com/roxana_barbulescu/6.

CHAPTER 7: BUILD YOUR AUDIENCE

1. Dorie Clark, "How to Attract the Right People to Your Life," *Forbes*, March 15, 2013. http://www.forbes.com/sites/dorieclark/2013/03/15/how-to-attract-the-right-people-to-your-life.
2. Dong Ngo, "Blogging Declines Among Teens, Young Adults," *CNET*, February 3, 2010. http://www.cnet.com/news/blogging-declines-among-teens-young-adults.
3. Margalit Fox, "Robert Zajonc, Who Looked at Mind's Ties to Actions, Is Dead at 85," *The New York Times*, December 6, 2008. http://www.nytimes.com/2008/12/07/education/07zajonc.html?_r=0.
4. Dorie Clark, "How to Become the Next Thought Leader," *Forbes*, March 14, 2013. http://www.forbes.com/sites/dorieclark/2013/03/14/how-to-become-the-next-thought-leader.
5. Dorie Clark, "Four Ways to Get Started as a Professional Speaker," LinkedIn Pulse, March 13, 2014. https://www.linkedin.com/today/post/article/20140313160127-5068349-four-ways-to-get-started-as-a-professional-speaker.

CHAPTER 8: BUILD A COMMUNITY

1. Joe Ciarallo, "Vocus Acquires Help a Reporter Out (HARO)," PRNewser, June 10, 2010. https://www.mediabistro.com/prnewser/vocus-acquires-help-a-reporter-out-haro_b3853.
2. Romain Dillet, "Adobe Acquired Portfolio Service Behance for More Than $150 Million in Cash and Stock," *TechCrunch*, December 12, 2012. http://techcrunch.com/2012/12/12/adobe-acquired-portfolio-service-behance-for-more-than-150-million-in-cash-and-stock.
3. "MBA Statistics," chart, Harvard Business School, 2014. http://www.hbs.edu/about/facts-and-figures/Pages/mba-statistics.aspx.
4. Seth Godin, "Applications Open for a Short Summer Internship," *Seth's Blog*, May 15, 2013. http://sethgodin.typepad.com/seths_blog/2013/05/seth-godin-internship.html.

CHAPTER 9: PUTTING THOUGHT LEADERSHIP INTO PRACTICE

1. Sean Silverthorne, "Time Pressure and Creativity: Why Time Is Not on Your Side," *Harvard Business School Working Knowledge*, July 29, 2002. http://hbswk.hbs.edu/item/3030.html.
2. Ibid.
3. Ap Dijksterhuis, "Think Different: The Merits of Unconscious Thought in Preference Development and Decision Making," *Journal of Personality and Social Psychology* 87 (5) (November 2004): 586–98. http://psycnet.apa.org/journals/psp/87/5/586.

4. Dorie Clark, "How to Attract the Right People to Your Life," *Forbes*, March 15, 2013. http://www.forbes.com/sites/dorieclark/2013/03/15/how-to-attract-the-right-people-to-your-life.
5. Dorie Clark, "How to Build a Lucky Network," *Forbes*, August 6, 2012. http://www.forbes.com/sites/dorieclark/2012/08/06/how-to-build-a-lucky-network.
6. I participated in Weiss's mentor program in early 2009.
7. Alan Weiss, "The Alan Card," Summit Consulting Group, 2014. http://summitconsulting.com/seminars/theAlanCard.php.
8. Dorie Clark, "How Raising Prices Can Increase Your Sales," *Forbes*, February 23, 2012. http://www.forbes.com/sites/dorieclark/2012/02/23/how-raising-prices-can-increase-your-sales.
9. Dorie Clark, "Why Gary Vaynerchuk's New Social Media Strategy Should Change the Way You Do Business," *Forbes*, June 5, 2013. http://www.forbes.com/sites/dorieclark/2013/06/05/why-gary-vaynerchuks-new-social-media-strategy-should-change-the-way-you-do-business.
10. Ben Carter, "Can 10,000 Hours of Practice Make You an Expert?" BBC, March 1, 2014. http://www.bbc.com/news/magazine-26384712.

INDEX